Georgetown Journal *of* International Affairs

Fall/Winter 2016, Volume XVII, number III

International Engagement on Cyber VI

Georgetown Journal *of* International Affairs

Fall/Winter 2016, Volume XVII, number III

International Engagement on Cyber VI

Georgetown Journal of International Affairs

Fall/Winter 2016, Volume XVII, number III

International Engagement on Cyber VI

Global Governance

Country in Focus

Safety & Security

Military Matters

Notice to Contributors

Articles submitted to the *Georgetown Journal of International Affairs* must be original, must not draw substantially from articles previously published by the author, and must not be simultaneously submitted to any other publication. Articles should be around 3,000 words in length. Manuscripts must be typewritten and double-spaced in Microsoft™ Word® format, with margins of at least one inch. Authors should follow the *Chicago Manual of Style*, 16th ed. Articles may be submitted by e-mail (gjia@georgetown.edu). Full names of authors, a two-sentence biography, and contact information including addresses with zip codes, telephone numbers, facsimile numbers, and e-mail addresses must accompany each submission. The *Georgetown Journal of International Affairs* will consider all manuscripts submitted but assumes no obligation regarding publication. All material submitted is returnable at the discretion of the *Georgetown Journal of International Affairs.*

The *Georgetown Journal of International Affairs* (ISSN 1526-0054; PB ISBN 978-1-62616-388-1) is published three times a year by Georgetown University Press for the Edmund A. Walsh School of Foreign Service, Georgetown University. Subscription rates for individuals: $39 for one year, $75 for two years, or $106 for three years. Subscription rates for institutions: $90 for one year or $176 for two years. Shipping and handling charges are not included. All subscriptions pay for 3 issues, including our annual cybersecurity feature issue.

Editorial and Advertising Office

Georgetown Journal of International Affairs
Edmund A. Walsh School of Foreign Service
Georgetown University
301 Intercultural Center
3700 O Street, NW
Washington, DC 20057
gjia@georgetown.edu

Subscriptions

Georgetown Journal of International Affairs
Subscriptions
c/o Johns Hopkins University Press
Journals Publishing Division
P.O. Box 19966
Baltimore, MD 21211-0966
Phone: 1-800-548-1784 or 410-516-6987
Fax: 410-516-3866
http://journal.georgetown.edu

Publisher

Georgetown University Press
3520 Prospect Street, NW
Suite 140
Washington, DC 20007
gupress@georgetown.edu

Backlist, Single-Copy, and Bulk Sales

Georgetown University Press
c/o Hopkins Fulfillment Service
P.O. Box 50370
Baltimore, MD 21211-4370
Phone: 1-800-537-5487 or 410-516-6965
Fax: 410-516-6998
www.press.georgetown.edu

The Georgetown Journal of International Affairs
would like to thank the following sponsors

Christiane Amanpour, American Broadcasting Company
Patrons Committee Chair

The Chrysler Foundation
Corporate Founding Sponsor

Patrons
The Richard Lounsbery Foundation
The Paul & Nancy Pelosi Charitable Foundation
Mr. Faul C. Besozzi

Friends
Mr. Jeremy Goldberg
Mr. Eric Peter
Mr. John Guy Van Benschoten
Mr. Pradeep Ramamurthy

To become a sponsor, contact
Edmund A. Walsh School of Foreign Service, Georgetown University
ICC 301, 3700 O St., NW, Washington, DC 20057
gjia@georgetown.edu

Editor's Note

The *Georgetown Journal of International Affairs* has once again partnered with Georgetown University's CyberProject to assemble articles from leading scholars, practitioners, and policymakers around the globe to publish the sixth special issue of *International Engagement on Cyber*. This special issue of the journal seeks to uncover timely topics, broaden the dialogue, and advance knowledge within the field of cyber.

In the Forum of this issue of *International Engagement on Cyber*, authors from academia, government, and the private sector evaluate the U.S. Department of Defense's 2015 Cyber Strategy and its efficacy in meeting cyber threats. Other topics covered in this issue include applying just war theory to the cyber capabilities of non-state actors including ISIS and Anonymous, litigating competing perspectives on the establishment of cyber norms, assessing tensions on the Korean peninsula in the cyber domain, and much more.

In presenting this sixth cyber issue, I offer my humble gratitude to our contributors and dedicated editorial staff, without whose work it would not have materialized. Sincere appreciation to Dr. Jennifer Long and Dr. Anthony Clark Arend, whose assistance exceeded the call of duty. Special gratitude also to Dr. Catherine Lotrionte, whose work remains our north star. To the readers: Enjoy.

Ian Prasad Philbrick

Forum: The Role of Strategy in Securing a Nation in the Cyber Domain

Introduction

Catherine Lotrionte and Anthony Clark Arend

When Georgetown University's School of Foreign Service was founded in 1919, it was a tumultuous time in world history. The First World War had just come to an end, the League of Nations was being created, and the United States was in a new position of prominence in the international system. The purpose of the school was to prepare people for this new uncertain and ever-changing world.

Today, as the school prepares to celebrate its centennial, the world is no less tumultuous. There are new actors and new forces in the international system, and the role of technology is unlike anything that could have been imagined in previous years. As the school prepares to address these challenges, one of the most important areas of concern is the cyber realm. In recognition of this challenge Georgetown University established the CyberProject in 2009. Each year since then we have convened the International Conference on Cyber Engagement. This conference brings together experts from the public, private, and nonprofit sectors from all over the world to analyze the most critical issues in the cyber realm and think creatively about ways to address problems.

One way that the CyberProject seeks to continue the conversation is through partnering with the *Georgetown Journal of International Affairs* on the publication of this annual special issue, *International Engagement on Cyber.*

The authors in this sixth special cyber issue bring a global view of some of the most troublesome aspects of cybersecurity that the international community faces. The Forum articles focus on the role of governments in formulating strategy to ensure the resiliency of the nation in the face of cyber attacks. The authors provide diverse perspectives on how states can ensure resilience from cyber attacks while balancing the constraints in-

Catherine Lotrionte is the executive director of the CyberProject in the Walsh School of Foreign Service at Georgetown University. **Anthony Clark Arend** is professor and senior associate dean for graduate and faculty affairs in the Walsh School of Foreign Service at Georgetown University.

herent in domestic regimes. Specifically, the Forum articles assess the current U.S. Department of Defense (DoD) Cyber Strategy and what it means for this country as it formulates an approach to defense and deterrence in the cyber domain. The authors' arguments deliver a diversity of perspectives, at times overlapping in their recommendations.

In 2015 DoD published its second cyber strategy to guide the development of DoD's cyber forces and strengthen its cyber defense and deterrence posture. The 2015 strategy outlines three cyber missions for DoD: to defend DoD's information network, to defend the United States against nationally significant cyber attacks, and to support conventional military operations with cyber capabilities. In his article, "Reflections on the New Department of Defense Cyber Strategy: What It Says, What It Doesn't Say," Herbert Lin explores the fundamental tenets of DoD's strategy. The author argues that the publication of the strategy is an important step in making this part of the public dialogue. But importantly, the author notes that the document does not address a series of critical issues, including the chain of command on the implementation of offensive cyber operations, the challenges of attribution, and the costs and benefits of using offensive cyber operations.

Robert Knake analyzes the new strategy and cautions against the assumption that DoD will be able to provide defensive support to the private sector in the United States. His article, "Respecting the Digital Rubicon: How the Department of Defense Should Defend the U.S. Homeland," assesses how DoD should carry out its mission within U.S. territory without destroying the democratic principles the country is based on. The author argues that the United States cannot assume that DoD has any greater capabilities than the private sector in protecting their assets and therefore recommends that security capabilities be commercialized instead of relying on DoD to operate the network defenses of private companies. The author concludes that the U.S. Department of Homeland Security, rather than DoD, ought to be the government entity that provides assistance to the private sector when necessary to protect its assets from cyber attacks while DoD serves in a supporting role.

Finally, in "The U.S. Department of Defense Cyber Strategy: A Call to Action for Partnership," Michele Myauo discusses how DoD's strategy highlights the need for a partnership between government, academia, and industry. The author argues that this partnership is key to the implementation of DoD's strategy and to the overall resiliency of U.S. cyber assets.

* * *

In March 2016 U.S. Secretary of Defense Ashton Carter testified that the United States has five key military challenges: China, Russia, North Korea, Iran, and terrorism. As the DoD Cyber Strategy sets forth, each of these threat actors has cyber capability—some more sophisticated than others, but all able to threaten the security of the nation. The risk of cyber attacks against the U.S. homeland is substantial, therefore, it is critically important that the United States and all states develop an appropriate strategy that identifies the role of different elements of the government and how they will operate together when a significant cyber incident against critical infrastructure cripples the nation's networks, systems, and information on which society depends. The articles in this issue challenge the reader to assess the role of government and society in ensuring the security of the nation and its cyber assets that are fundamentally important to the modern way of life.

Reflections on the New Department of Defense Cyber Strategy

What It Says, What It Doesn't Say

Herbert S. Lin

In April 2015, U.S. Secretary of Defense Ash Carter unveiled the new cyber strategy of the U.S. Department of Defense (DoD). In his speech at Stanford University, he described three missions in the cyber domain for the DoD:

> The first is defending our own networks and weapons, because they're critical to what we do every day. . . . Second, we help defend the nation against cyberattacks from abroad—especially if they would cause loss of life, property destruction, or significant foreign policy and economic consequences. And our third mission is to provide offensive cyber options that, if directed by the President, can augment our other military systems.[1]

He noted that the DoD would respond to cyber threats as it did to more conventional threats. That is, the DoD prefers to deter malicious action before it occurs and wishes to be able to defend against incoming attacks, but in both cases the DoD is willing to exercise offensive options if necessary.

The publication of the DoD Cyber Strategy (hereafter, "the strategy")[2] reveals a great deal about how the United States is thinking about using cyber operations—especially offensive cyber operations—in support of its primary mission of providing the military forces needed to deter war and protecting the security of the United States.[3] This is especially true when the strategy is seen in the context of Carter's speech and Presidential Policy Directive 20 (PPD-20), leaked by Edward Snowden and described in a number of news articles.[4] Of course, "a great deal" in this context is a relative term—much about the U.S. acquisition and use of offensive cyber capabilities remains classified, so much so that information needed for an informed discussion about this topic is too often scarce.

This article is primarily focused on what the new DoD strategy says and does not say about cyber offense.

The Intended Effects of DoD Offensive Operations in Cyberspace

The strategy is silent on the specific effects that offensive cyber capabilities are intended to cause. But according to the *Guardian*, PPD-20—a document that pertains mostly (but not entirely) to certain non-intelligence cyber activities of the U.S. government—defines "Offensive Cyber Effects Operations" as the use of cyber weapons for "manipulation, disruption, denial, degradation, or destruction" of "physical or virtual" computer systems.

The emphasis on such effects is consistent with a long-standing distinction drawn by cyber analysts between cyber operations

Herbert S. Lin is senior research scholar for cyber policy and security at the Center for International Security and Cooperation and research fellow at the Hoover Institution, both at Stanford University. He is also chief scientist, emeritus for the Computer Science and Telecommunications Board at the National Research Council of the National Academies, where he served from 1990 to 2014.

for attack (that is, for manipulation, disruption, denial, degradation, or destruction) and those for exploitation.[5] Operations for exploitation collect information for foreign intelligence purposes and are governed by provisions of Title 50 of the U.S. Code, which governs activities of the intelligence community. By contrast, operations for attack are under most circumstances governed by provisions of Title 10 of the U.S. Code, which governs activities of the DoD.[6]

Targeting of DoD Offensive Operations in Cyberspace

For the first time, the DoD is explicit about some of the military sets of offensive cyber operations: "If directed, DoD should be able to use cyber operations to disrupt an adversary's command and control networks, military-related critical infrastructure, and weapons capabilities." This statement is comparable in significance to the authoritative congressional testimony of the DoD in 1980, describing the four principal target groups for U.S. nuclear weapons.[7]

Two observations are relevant with respect to this statement about targeting of offensive cyber operations. First, the possible uses of offensive cyber operations are not limited to the examples provided. Second, the possibility of targeting military-related infrastructure raises the possibility that the infrastructure may be of a dual-use character (that is, may have both civilian and military uses) and that planning for offensive cyber operations against such infrastructure may have to account for possible collateral damage to civilian interests. This point is consistent with the long-standing view in U.S doctrine that war-supporting infrastructure constitutes a valid military target under the Geneva Conventions, but this view is not universally held.

Anticipated Uses of Offensive Cyber Capabilities

As with other offensive capabilities available to military forces, offensive cyber capabilities can be used for defensive purposes and for offensive purposes.

Cyber Offense in Support of Cyber Defense

In regard to defending U.S. national interests in cyberspace, the strategy notes that the DoD has developed "capabilities for cyber operations and is integrating those capabilities into the full array of tools that the United States government uses to defend U.S. national interests, including diplomatic, informational, military, economic, financial, and law enforcement tools." Integrating cyber capabilities into the full array of tools available to the U.S. government is not new, but it is a point worth underscoring in light of the common but mistaken presumption that hostile cyber activity against U.S. national interests necessitates a cyber response from the United States.

The strategy also adds a welcome nuance to the scope of DoD responsibilities for defense in cyberspace. It states that the "DoD must be prepared to defend the United States and its interests against cyberattacks of significant consequence . . . [which] may include loss of life, significant damage to property, serious adverse U.S. foreign policy consequences, or serious economic impact on the United States." Put differently, the DoD accepts responsibility only for defending against cyber attacks that are in the top 2 percent of consequence.[8]

This statement implies at least two interesting and interrelated questions. First, who decides when a given attack is of significant consequence to warrant DoD involvement? The strategy says that "cyberattacks are assessed on a case-by-case and fact-specific basis by the President and the U.S. national security team." This cannot be true for all cyber attacks on the United States—there are far too many attacks for the president and his national security team to address.[9] So only a fraction of these attacks can rise to the level of presidential attention.

Second, how should lower-level decision makers know when to bring any given attack to the attention of a higher authority? Section 313 of the House-passed version of the Intelligence Authorization Act for Fiscal Year 2016 directs the director of national intelligence to determine standards for measuring the damage of cyber incidents for the purpose of determining the response to such incidents, including a method for quantifying the damage caused to affected computers, systems, and devices.[10] If such standards existed, bringing a cyber incident to the attention of a higher authority might simply be a matter of establishing a minimum threshold for such attention. It is nevertheless true that reliable and useful metrics for security have eluded cybersecurity researchers for many years, and the technical feasibility of such metrics remains to be seen.

How the U.S. government will decide when a given cyber attack warrants presidential attention is thus uncertain at this time.

Lastly, the DoD reserves the right, with appropriate National Command Authority, to launch offensive operations in cyberspace in anticipation of "an imminent or on-going attack against the U.S. homeland or U.S. interests in cyberspace, [with] the purpose of . . . blunt[ing] an attack and prevent[ing] the destruction of property or the loss of life." The strategy notes that "the United States will seek to exhaust all network defense and law enforcement options to mitigate any potential cyber risk to the U.S. homeland or U.S. interests before conducting a[n offensive] cyberspace operation," but this reservation is consistent with long-standing U.S. interpretations of the laws of war that nations have the right to take action in the face of imminent attacks.[11]

The use of offensive capabilities in the manner described previously is usually captured under the rubric of "active defense" or, in some formulations, computer network defense response action. In general, such actions are tactical activities used as a last resort in response to a specific hostile activity and are designed to address and mitigate that activity, and only that activity. One example of a response action could be an offensive operation to shut down a botnet controller that is directing an attack on DoD cyber assets in cyberspace.[12]

Cyber Offense in Support of National Objectives

In the most significant new statement in the strategy, it is noted:

> DoD must be able to provide integrated cyber capabilities to support military operations and contingency plans. There may be times when the President or the Secretary of Defense may determine that it would be appropriate for the U.S. military to conduct cyber operations to disrupt an adversary's military-related networks or infrastructure so that the U.S. military can protect U.S. interests in an area of operations. For example, the United States military might use cyber operations to terminate an ongoing conflict on U.S. terms, or to disrupt an adversary's military systems to prevent the use of force against U.S. interests.

Another part of the strategy states:

> DoD should be able to use cyber operations to disrupt an adversary's command and control networks, military-related critical infrastructure, and weapons capabilities. As

> a part of the full range of tools available to the United States, DoD must develop viable cyber options and integrate those options into Departmental plans. DoD will develop cyber capabilities to achieve key security objectives with precision, and to minimize loss of life and destruction of property. To ensure unity of effort, DoD will enable combatant commands to plan and synchronize cyber operations with kinetic operations across all domains of military operations.

The most significant aspect of this statement is that the DoD is not restricting the exercise of its offensive cyber capabilities to retaliatory action for hostile cyber activity, but rather for use as general-purpose warfighting tools—according to the *Guardian*, such capabilities can be used broadly to advance "U.S. national objectives around the world."

Furthermore, the DoD sometimes places its conventional military assets at the disposal of the intelligence community to support covert action, such as Operation Neptune Spear, in which assets from the Navy and Army (SEAL team and helicopters, respectively) used in the mission were under the operational control of the Central Intelligence Agency (CIA).[13] In this context, it is noteworthy that the strategy states that U.S. Cyber Command "may also be directed to conduct [offensive] cyber operations, in coordination with other U.S. government agencies as appropriate, to deter or defeat strategic threats in other domains." Thus, to the extent that CIA covert operations might call for the exercise of offensive cyber operations (and indeed, it is hard to imagine instruments that are more suitable for the conduct of [deniable] covert action than cyber weapons[14]), U.S. Cyber Command may be involved in such action.

Offensive Operations in Cyberspace on the Escalation Ladder

The strategy states that "during heightened tensions or outright hostilities, DoD must be able to provide the President with a wide range of options for managing conflict escalation." Note the reference to periods of "heightened tension"—by definition, periods of heightened tension are pre-conflict, suggesting that offensive cyber operations may *precede* the outbreak of outright hostilities. In other words, offensive cyber operations are at the bottom of the escalation ladder—they are (or can be) pre-kinetic.[15]

The logic of offensive cyber operations also suggests their early use. When overt conflict breaks out, the various sides involved are likely to strengthen their defensive postures, including their cyber defenses. Such actions may eliminate paths for access or system vulnerabilities that an offensive operation might have used.

Finally, operational preparation of the cyber battlefield (OPB) is likely to be an ongoing activity as routine as peacetime reconnaissance or surveillance of potential adversary activity. OPB involves an active search for vulnerabilities in and access paths to adversary systems and networks and, when possible, implantation of "hooks" that will later facilitate overtly destructive cyber action should such action be necessary. The key characteristic of OPB is that it is not, in itself, a destructive act in any way, though it is not a friendly one either.

The Attribution of Hostile Cyber Operations

The strategy states that "attribution is a fundamental part of an effective cyber deterrence strategy as anonymity enables malicious cyber activity by state and non-state groups" and further notes significant investments in "all source collection, analysis, and dissemination capabilities, all of which reduce the anonymity of state and non-state actor activity in cyberspace. Intelligence and attribution capabilities help to unmask an actor's cyber persona, identify the attack's point of origin, and determine tactics, techniques, and procedures."

In short, the document asserts that attribution is an essential element of deterrence and that the attribution task is not hopeless. Although nearly everyone would concur with the first point, the second is more controversial. Many observers argue that definitive attribution of hostile cyber operations is impossible, since actual perpetrators can plant or forge technical evidence pointing the finger at other parties.

But this latter point of view—at least in its strong form—is wrong.[16] Fundamentally, attribution is a judgment call that takes into account many different kinds of information. Technical evidence is one, but only one, source, and the DoD and the intelligence community derive useful information from multiple sources. Such sources can include but are not limited to human intelligence (e.g., spies), signals intelligence (e.g., monitored phone calls or e-mails), and open source intelligence (e.g., newspaper stories). Furthermore, because perpetrators sometimes engage in hostile cyber activities repeatedly, similarities between current activities and previous activities may be suggestive. Geopolitical context (e.g., are significant disputes between two nations ongoing?) also matters.

No one source of information is ever definitive for an attribution judgment. But multiple sources, taken together and most pointing in the same direction, do increase confidence in attribution judgments. On the other hand, integrating such information usually takes time, and so prompt or near-real-time high-confidence attribution is indeed hard or impossible under many or most circumstances.

The strategy also indicates that private-sector parties (e.g., security firms) reporting on attribution "can play a significant role in dissuading cyber actors from conducting attacks in the first place." Such reports are usually unclassified in their entirety, which means that they can be used by government officials in responding to questions about the attribution of any given cyber incident.

One major advantage of private-sector attribution is the potential increase in analytical and collection resources that can be brought to bear on tracing the origin of hostile cyber operations. Additional resources will be necessary as the volume of hostile cyber operations conducted by "activist groups, criminal organizations, and other actors acquire advanced cyber capabilities" increases.

A second advantage is that sensitive sources and methods of government intelligence collection are not revealed in private-sector attribution reports. Third, government responsibility for an attribution judgment is attenuated when the actual judgment is made by a private party, even if government authorities point unofficially to that analysis when questioned about a given incident. Attenuated responsibility may yield diplomatic benefits.

But there are disadvantages as well. For example, private-sector attribution reports are valuable marketing tools that elevate the authoring firms in the public eye. The incentives motivating these firms to produce such reports may degrade the quality of their research and analysis.

In addition, reports from the private sector are not subject to independent oversight and quality control. The private-sector security market is robust enough to provide some independent scrutiny, and since each firm has its professional reputation to uphold, they all have incentives to produce high-quality work. Whether market forces are sufficient to uphold quality in such reports remains to be seen.

Finally, given the semipermeable membrane between private-sector security firms and government authorities, it would not be surprising if from time to time, government officials talking to their colleagues in the private sector suggest that looking for X rather than Y in their investigative efforts could prove more fruitful. That is, such reports may be produced with some measure of government input, even if such input is not apparent.

The Authority to Execute "Significant" Offensive Cyber Operations and Integration of Cyber Operations with Other Aspects of Military Power

The strategy notes that the military needs explicit direction from the National Command Authority (NCA) to conduct offensive cyber operations for (a) "counter[ing] an imminent or on-going attack against the U.S. homeland or U.S. interests in cyberspace"; and (b) "support[ing] military operations and contingency plans" for, for example, "disrupt[ing] an adversary's military-related networks or infrastructure so that the U.S. military can protect U.S. interests in an area of operations."

The fact that such authorization is explicitly required for such uses of offensive cyber operations places them in the same category as the use of nuclear or antisatellite weapons. These three categories of action share the characteristic that they are widely recognized as actions with high potential to escalate rather than de-escalate a conflict. In the case of cyber, escalatory potential arises from many factors, including a lack of knowledge about connectivity in adversary systems and networks, about how effects might propagate, and about how an adversary might perceive such use. For example, a cyber attack intended for tactical purposes could run the risk of being perceived as an attack for strategic purposes. Offensive cyber operations also have the potential to precipitate overt conflict, especially since they are a pre-conflict option as described in Section 0. In the face of such uncertainty, it is natural that decisions with significant escalatory potential would be made at the highest levels of the U.S. government.

On the other hand, the strategy also states:

> As a part of the full range of tools available to the United States, DoD must develop viable cyber options and integrate those options into Departmental plans. . . . To ensure unity of effort, DoD will enable combatant commands to plan and synchronize cyber operations with kinetic operations across all domains of military operations.

That is, the DoD intends to integrate offensive cyber operations into its operational practices. Two aspects of this integration are noteworthy. First, cyber weapons are to be treated as just another option available to combatant commands. In principle, the advantages and disadvantages of cyber weapons compared to other weapons in any given scenario will be assessed, and when this assessment suggests the use of cyber weapons is preferable, they will be used. Second, the DoD intends that the habits of thought and the intellectual constructs that characterize operational planning for using other weapons will also be applied to cyber operations.

The desire to integrate offensive cyber operations into the DoD kit bag stands in some contrast to the authorities for conducting cyber operations described earlier. That is, an instrument that is intended for routine use like other military instruments also requires explicit NCA authorization before it can be used, at least in some cases.

Building and Maintaining International Alliances

The strategy notes that all three of the DoD's cyber missions—including that of providing offensive cyber options for decision makers—require collaboration with foreign allies and partners, and thus the DoD "seeks to build partnership capacity in cybersecurity and cyber defense, and to deepen operational partnerships where appropriate."

To build partnerships related to traditional military capabilities, the United States has used many instruments over the years, including the Foreign Military Sales (FMS) program and other programs "specifically designed to address and expedite international partners' urgent or emerging requirements or capability gaps."[17] The Defense Security and Cooperation Agency of the DoD is responsible for the transfer of defense articles and services to approved partners via sale, lease, or grant, in furtherance of U.S. national security and foreign policy objectives.

Speaking generally, export controls have long been used to stem the proliferation of certain "dangerous" technologies, that is, technologies that would be dangerous were they to fall into the hands of adversaries. The United States controls the export of defense articles and defense services. Defense articles and services are those intended explicitly and primarily for military use and thus do not fall into the "dual-use" category. Regulated defense articles and services are found on the U.S. Munitions List (USML).[18]

The items on the USML do not explicitly include cyber weapons.[19] However, Category 21 of the USML (miscellaneous items) is a catchall category for items not otherwise enumerated, and the decision on whether any specific article is included in this category is made by the director or Office of Defense Trade Controls Policy. To the extent that transfers of cyber weapons or components thereof (e.g., payloads targeted against weapon systems[20]) are covered under the USML, it is likely that they are captured under the auspices of Category 21.[21]

Given that various other nations have benefitted from a long history of U.S. transfers of defense articles and services, it would not be surprising if they seek to obtain offensive cyber capabilities for military use from the U.S. government in the future. The strategy is, however, silent on this topic, suggesting the need to develop a policy regarding the facts and circumstances that would warrant transfers of such capabilities to another nation.

Discussion and Conclusion

The discussion contained in the 2015 DoD Cyber Strategy regarding U.S. offensive capabilities in cyberspace is a major step forward in the national conversation about how the DoD will use cyberspace to support its mission. But beyond the published strategy document, what should DoD be saying about its strategy in cyberspace? Here are a few illustrative examples of important question topics on which the strategy is silent:

- How and to what extent, if any, is authority to order the use of offensive cyber operations delegated down the military chain of command?
- Given that attribution of a hostile cyber attack may be delayed in time, what is the impact of that delay on the scope and nature of a U.S. response to that attack, and how does that affect the deterrent value of any such response?
- What circumstances, if any, require prompt attribution for an effective U.S. response?

- What is the impact of operational preparation of the cyber battlefield on adversary perceptions of U.S. intentions, especially during times of crises?
- What factors and trade-offs drive decisions to use—or not use—offensive cyber capabilities in various operational scenarios?

It is not a criticism in any way of the strategy that it does not address these questions: a 33-page document cannot express the totality of DoD thinking on such matters. Still, these and other questions naturally emerge in pondering the implications of the strategy document, and we can only hope that future DoD reports on cyber strategy and other authoritative DoD publications will continue to make even more information available.

Acknowledgements

I thank Edward Geist (Stanford University) and Thomas Berson (Anagram Laboratories) for helpful comments and insights.

Notes

1. Ashton Carter, "Remarks by Secretary Carter at the Drell Lecture, Cemex Auditorium, Stanford Graduate School of Business, Stanford, California," U.S. Department of Defense, April 23, 2015, http://www.defense.gov/News/News-Transcripts/Transcript-View/Article/607043.
2. U.S. Department of Defense, "The DOD Cyber Strategy," April 2015, http://www.defense.gov/Portals/1/features/2015/0415_cyber-strategy/Final_2015_DoD_CYBER_STRATEGY_for_web.pdf.
3. U.S. Department of Defense, "About the Department of Defense (DoD)," accessed April 5, 2016, http://www.defense.gov/About-DoD.
4. The leaked PPD-20 can be read in full at https://fas.org/irp/offdocs/ppd/ppd-20.pdf. It has also been the subject of several news articles and editorials, including Glenn Greenwald and Ewen MacAskill, "Obama Orders U.S. to Draw Up Overseas Target List for Cyber-Attacks," *Guardian*, June 7, 2013, http://www.theguardian.com/world/2013/jun/07/obama-china-targets-cyber-overseas; Editorial Board, "Cyberwar: The White House Is Thinking Ahead," *Washington Post*, June 16, 2013, https://www.washingtonpost.com/opinions/cyberwar-the-white-house-is-thinking-ahead/2013/06/16/b4a0ab00-d4fa-11e2-a73e-826d299ff459_story.html; Bill Gertz, "Cyber War Details Revealed," *Washington Free Beacon*, June 11, 2013, http://freebeacon.com/national-security/cyber-war-details-revealed/; and Mark Clayton, "Presidential Cyberwar Directive Gives Pentagon Long-Awaited Marching Orders," *Christian Science Monitor*, June 10, 2013, http://www.csmonitor.com/USA/Military/2013/0610/Presidential-cyberwar-directive-gives-Pentagon-long-awaited-marching-orders-video. Because those with clearances are allowed to read press stories reporting on leaked classified documents but not to read these documents themselves outside cleared facilities, references to PPD-20 in this article should be understood as being derived from these articles and not from the original document.
5. See, for example, JP3-12(R), *Cyberspace Operations*, Joint Chiefs of Staff, February 5, 2013, http://www.dtic.mil/doctrine/new_pubs/jp3_12R.pdf, I-5.
6. The primary exception to this point is that covert actions involving cyber attacks would be governed under Title 50 because covert actions are by Executive Order 12333 the responsibility of the intelligence community.
7. US SASC DOD Authorization for Appropriations for FY 1981, US GPO, Part 5, 2721. In 1980 these four target groups were the Soviet nuclear forces, the general purpose forces, the Soviet military and political leadership centers, and the Soviet economic and industrial base.
8. See the congressional testimony of Eric Rosenbach (then assistant secretary of de-

fense for homeland defense and global security) in anticipation of the strategy's release, http://www.armed-services.senate.gov/imo/media/doc/Rosenbach_04-14-15.pdf. See also Tyrone C. Marshall Jr., "New DoD Cyber Strategy Nears Release, Official Says," U.S. Department of Defense, April 14, 2015, http://www.defense.gov/News-Article-View/Article/604456.

9. For example, in the nine months between September 2014 and June 2015, DoD networks alone experienced 30 million malicious intrusions. Less than 0.1 percent of these intrusions resulted in a compromised system—even so, that figure represents as many as 30,000 compromises. See Department of Defense, *Cybersecurity Culture and Compliance Initiative*, Memorandum for Secretaries of the Military Departments, September 3, 2015, http://www.defense.gov/Portals/1/Documents/pubs/OSD011517-15-RES-Final.pdf, 1.
10. U.S. House of Representatives, Intelligence Authorization Act for Fiscal Year 2016, H.R. 4127, 114th Cong. (2015), https://www.congress.gov/114/bills/hr4127/BILLS-114hr4127pcs.pdf.
11. See, for example, sec. 1.11.5.1, DoD Law of War Manual, June 2015, http://www.defense.gov/Portals/1/Documents/DoD_Law_of_War_Manual-June_2015_Updated_May_2016.pdf.
12. William Owens, Kenneth Dam, and Herbert Lin, eds., *Technology, Policy, Law, and Ethics Regarding U.S. Acquisition and Use of Cyberattack Capabilities* (Washington, DC: National Academies Press, 2009), 170.
13. Nate Rawlings, "*Operation Neptune Spear*: The New Textbook for Special Operators," *Time,* May 2, 2012, http://nation.time.com/2012/05/02/operation-neptune-spear-the-new-textbook-for-special-operators/.
14. Owens, Dam, and Lin, *Technology, Policy, Law, and Ethics*, p. 50 and sec. 4.3.
15. A good discussion of offensive operations in cyberspace as they relate to kinetic conflict, especially in times of crisis, can be found at Martin C. Libicki, *Crisis and Escalation in Cyberspace*, Rand Corporation and Project Air Force, 2012, http://www.rand.org/content/dam/rand/pubs/monographs/2012/RAND_MG1215.pdf.
16. For some more nuanced views of attribution, see, for example, Thomas Rid and Ben Buchanan, "Attributing Cyber Attacks," *Journal of Strategic Studies* 38, no. 1–2 (2015): 4–37, http://www.tandfonline.com/doi/pdf/10.1080/01402390.2014.977382; and David D. Clark and Susan Landau, "Untangling Attribution," in *Proceedings of a Workshop on Deterring Cyberattacks: Informing Strategies and Developing Options for U.S. Policy*, National Research Council, 25–40 (Washington, DC: National Academies Press, 2010).
17. See the Defense Security Cooperation Agency website, http://www.dsca.mil/.
18. United States Munitions List, 22 CFR Ch. 1, part 121 (4-1-13 ed.), https://www.pmddtc.state.gov/regulations_laws/documents/official_itar/ITAR_Part_121.pdf.
19. The USML does include as restricted items military cryptanalytic systems, equipment, assemblies, modules, integrated circuits, components or software that would enhance an adversary's signals intelligence capabilities.
20. In general, a cyber weapon requires both penetration and payload. The penetration mechanism is used to gain access to the target system of interest and takes advantage of a vulnerability in the system. The payload is the mechanism for affecting the victim's system or network after penetration has occurred. Penetration mechanisms (but not payloads) are regulated as dual-use items as described in note 21.
21. Another category of export-restricted items is that of dual-use information technology artifacts, that is, artifacts with both civilian and military purposes. Such dual-use items are not classified as munitions, and the export of such items is regulated by the Department of Commerce under the provisions of the Wassenaar Arrangement.

Respecting the Digital Rubicon

How the Department of Defense Should Defend the U.S. Homeland

Rob K. Knake

The U.S. Department of Defense (DoD) Cyber Strategy is a model for clear writing and thinking on cybersecurity. Unlike earlier DoD strategies, gone is tone-deaf language about "dominating" cyberspace. Instead, the strategy recognizes an important but limited role for the DoD in the security of cyberspace. The strategy divides that role into three missions: (1) defense of the DoD Information Network (DoDIN); (2) defense of the United States against nationally significant cyber attacks; and (3) conduct of cyber operations in support of conventional military operations.

How the DoD fulfills the first and third missions is clear given what the strategy says (and does not say). Cyber Protection Forces will carry out the first mission; their role is pure network defense. In turn, the Combat Mission Forces will engage in cyber operations in support of military operations around the world. Their role is pure offense. In between the two is the second mission. Per the strategy, defending the United States in cyberspace is the job of the National Mission Forces. Yet, how the National Mission Forces will carry out their mission is left unanswered by the strategy. Many pundits assume that the answer will be a mixture of offense and defense—assisting private companies with network defense as well as conducting offensive operations to stop cyber attacks that overwhelm these defenses. While the DoD has a monopoly on offensive operations, the assumption that the DoD will also provide defensive support to the private sector is problematic. It could lead the DoD down a dangerous path, one that could upset long-standing traditions on the respective roles of civilian and military organizations in our democracy.

Teasing Out the Role of the National Mission Forces

The DoD's intentions for how the National Mission Forces will carry out its mission are hard to divine from the strategy. The strategy makes clear that the role of the Cyber Protection Forces is what is traditionally considered network defense. In all, the strategy spends over four pages on defense of the DoDIN, delineating 15 tasks and 16 subtasks under this mission area. Cyber Protection Teams have a mission to "discover, detect, analyze, and mitigate threats and vulnerabilities to defend the DoD information network." Their role is network defense, taking place on the DoDIN, not off it. When discussing the offensive mission, the strategy is noticeably and reasonably more circumspect and circumscribed, devoting only a couple of bullets to it. What the strategy does make clear is that the Combat Mission Forces are an offensive component, as their name implies, that takes the fight to adversary networks.

For the National Mission Forces, the

Rob K. Knake is the Whitney Shepardson senior fellow at the Council on Foreign Relations, where his work centers on Internet governance, public-private partnerships, and cyber conflict. He is also an adjunct lecturer at Georgetown University's McCourt School of Public Policy and a senior advisor to the machine learning company Context Relevant. From 2011 to 2015, he served as director for cybersecurity policy at the National Security Council.

strategy signals a hybrid mission—it is a hodgepodge of both offensive and defensive language. The National Mission Forces are meant to develop "capabilities to mitigate sophisticated, malicious cyberattacks *before* [emphasis added] they can impact U.S. interests." This emphasis on preemption may indicate that the role of the National Mission Forces will be to conduct offensive operations in defense of U.S. networks; however, it could also imply a network defense mission to block attacks before they cause harm. The idea that the DoD should operate defenses for the private sector has proved to be unworkable, yet the strategy does not definitively rule out this role, leading many watchers of cyber policy to conclude that Cyber Command will only be a phone call away to assist with cleaning up intrusions and stopping follow-on attacks.

The assumption that the National Mission Forces will have a defensive role is based on two faulty premises: first, that the DoD has network defense capabilities that exceed those of the private sector; and second, that the government recognizes a responsibility to provide network defenses to private companies being targeted by national adversaries. Neither is true. The best network defense teams in the private sector are as good, if not better, than their DoD counterparts; moreover, while the DoD has strong capabilities, it does not have extensive capacity. Private-sector capabilities are available for purchase and therefore subject to market forces rather than congressional action in determining how quickly these capabilities grow.

Any attempt by the DoD to provide network defense capability to private companies will undermine the significant effort undertaken by the Obama administration to convince private companies that it is in their interest to address cyber threats on their own terms rather than by having government either dictate standards or directly intervene and provide network protection.

Attempting to scale the DoD's network defense operations to cover vast swaths of the economy, if it could be done effectively, would undermine private investment in cybersecurity. Bringing the military into the domestic realm would also raise significant privacy and civil liberties concerns and violate long-standing traditions in American civic life. Instead, the National Mission Forces should have a singular focus on developing the capability to deter and disrupt nationally significant attacks through the use of offensive operations when network defense and law enforcement action are ineffective.

The Pitfalls of a National Protection System

While the strategy provides little detail on how the National Mission Forces might provide defensive support to the private sector, the thinking behind the strategy has been made public. In a seminal 2010 piece in *Foreign Affairs*, then–deputy secretary of defense Bill Lynn set out how the DoD would defend the nation in cyberspace. He began by describing how the DoD defends its networks. "The National Security Agency has pioneered systems that, using warnings provided by U.S. intelligence capabilities, automatically deploy defenses to counter intrusions in real time," he wrote. "Part sensor, part sentry, part sharpshooter," he continued, "these active defense systems represent a fundamental shift in the U.S. approach to network defense."[1] Lynn explained that this technology is placed at the points of presence where military networks connect with the Internet and block attacks before getting inside the DoDIN.

Lynn went on to raise the possibility that the protection system the Pentagon developed for its own network should be used to protect the rest of the United States in cyberspace. "Policymakers," he wrote, "need to consider, among other things, applying the National Security Agency's defense capabilities beyond the '.gov' domain." That was the idea behind the National Cybersecurity Protection System, the overarching program under which the much maligned Department of Homeland Security (DHS) Einstein program falls. While initially focused on providing protection to federal agencies, the program has a name, the National Cybersecurity Protection System, that implies a grander vision. Yet given the difficulties in deploying the system to federal agencies, well documented by the Government Accountability Office,[2] the technical, legal, and policy hurdles to the government deploying the system to the private sector likely cannot be overcome even if the political environment created the appetite to do so.

Writing in 2010, Lynn could not have predicted the political environment that the Snowden revelations would create some three years later. In 2016 the Federal Bureau of Investigation could not muster better than 50 percent public support for forcing Apple to assist in gaining access to the data on a phone owned by the employer of a deceased terrorist. Today, the idea of allowing the National Security Agency (NSA) to police domestic networks for cybersecurity purposes is almost laughable. Furthermore, the advantage that Lynn cites for NSA's technology over commercial solutions no longer holds true.

The use of "government intelligence capabilities to provide highly specialized active defenses" in 2010 could potentially give network defenders a chance against malware that was not known to the commercial world of signature writers. Today, stopping new malware does not require "using warnings provided by U.S. intelligence capabilities" but signatureless detection systems that identify anomalies in how files are executed and in network traffic patterns. Solutions are sold by companies like FireEye, Palo Alto Networks, Fidelis, and others.

In the summer of 2015, the DoD's defense system went up against an alleged Russian adversary. It lost. In August of that year, the DoD disclosed that the unclassified e-mail system of the Joint Chiefs of Staff had been hacked. The attack, attributed to Russia by a Pentagon spokesperson, was said to be "sophisticated." Yet in one respect, it was fairly routine: the attack began with a spear-phishing e-mail. In response, the Pentagon shut down the system for two weeks, leaving 4,000 staff members without access to unclassified e-mail systems.

The Pentagon deserves credit for quick detection and isolation of the incident. Yet the incident is instructive for those who would hope that the Pentagon has all the answers this nation needs on cybersecurity. The Pentagon's network defense sensors clearly failed to identify and stop both the spear-phishing e-mail and the malware used to infect and take over the e-mail system. Instead, it was detected after the malware had been installed and was engaging in some form of anomalous activity that the Pentagon's intrusion analysts were able to detect.

What this event suggests is that the capabilities the Pentagon can bring to network defense are no doubt very good but also that they are not far and away above solutions developed by private companies. If the Pentagon has yet to crack the code of spear-phishing, which would force adversaries like the Russians to identify and exploit remotely executed vulnerabilities, the Cyber Protection Teams are still wrestling with the same set of problems the rest of the community also has yet to solve. While it may be appealing to hope that the Pentagon could deploy its sensors on the networks of private companies or on the backbone of the Internet and filter out malicious traffic before it reaches its intended victim, there is nothing to suggest that these capabilities would be better than those that private companies can buy on their own.

If in fact these systems did provide capabilities that the private sector needed to defend against advanced adversaries, the civil liberties implications of the DoD operating them would be enormous. To stop malicious activity on the Internet, you first need to monitor for it. Any system, whether established nationally to cover all traffic or only for enclaves behind which companies would be protected, would need to be able to scan all traffic, thus requiring that the traffic be unencrypted at the location of the sensor. The growing ubiquity of encryption would render these systems useless unless the DoD were able to mandate that it be provided clear text so its systems could read every e-mail that crosses the networks they protect for signs of spear-phishing and examine every packet for malware.

Given these concerns, a better solution than having the DoD operate network defense for the private sector would be to commercialize the capability. That is in fact the approach that the DoD took in 2012, when, in a partnership with DHS and managed security service providers, it allowed private companies to buy security services that incorporate classified signatures provided by intelligence agencies through a program called Enhanced Cybersecurity Services.[3] Thus far, interest in the program is reported to be low. The strategy references Enhanced Cybersecurity Services but does not definitively and categorically rule out operating network defenses for the private sector itself.

Cyber Command as a Supporting Actor

The hacking of the Joint Chiefs e-mail system is a reminder that effective cybersecurity cannot be done at the network perimeter, but instead requires the ability to identify and contain malicious activity inside the network. Lynn identified the ability to "hunt" within the Pentagon's own networks as a critical capability for when perimeter approaches fail. In the commercial market today, hunting for threats is the latest craze. Companies are recognizing that every endpoint must become a sensor inside their network for detecting malicious activity, that they must monitor "east-west" flows of data within their networks, and that they must store and process log data to conduct forensics on intruder activity. All this activity takes dedicated time, resources, and knowledge of a company's network. If operating perimeter network defenses is not a viable option for the National Mission Forces to fulfill their mission, can they at least provide support to help ferret out threats inside private networks?

The strategy certainly contemplates that part of the DoD's mission to assist the private sector in protecting itself as part of Defense Support to Civil Authorities (DSCA). The problem with relying on the DoD's hunt teams to assist private companies is one of scale and incentives. While much has been made of Cyber Command's plans to grow its personnel to 6,200, this is a relatively small number of people in a field that currently has 250,000 job openings. The number of job openings in the field is expected to grow fourfold in the next five years. Moreover, the National Mission Forces is expected to be a fraction of the total force size.

In a 2015 interview with *Defense One*, Lt. Col. Valerie Henderson, a spokesperson for Cyber Command, broke down how the 6,200 personnel would be deployed among the three force components. Nearly half (2,720) will go to the Cyber Protection Teams; 1,600 will be on the Combat Mission Teams; the remainder, only 780, is planned for the National Mission Teams.[4] For perspective, the CEO of JP Morgan, Jamie Dimon, has committed to building his company's cybersecurity staff to 1,000 people. With so few resources, the National Mission Teams will be forced to selectively choose which private companies receive free cybersecurity services from the government; in so doing, they will compete with private companies that offer these same services on the open market and undermine the push to make the private sector absorb the costs of cybersecurity. As Mark Weatherford, former deputy undersecretary for cybersecurity at DHS, has put it, "The government is not going to come riding in on a white horse to rescue you when you have a security incident."[5] Ironically, DoD's positioning on the role of the National Mission Teams may undermine investments in cybersecurity by private companies, thereby leaving the nation less secure in cyberspace.

Offense in Support of Defense

If the DoD should not play a role in network defense, what then is Cyber Command's role in defending the homeland? As in other areas of defense policy, the role of the military is to defend the homeland from foreign attacks by projecting power abroad, not by policing our cities or the networks of fiber and copper that connect them. Rather than operate firewalls and intrusion prevention systems for the private sector or provide advice on how to do so, Cyber Command should train, plan, and equip to use its offensive capabilities when defense is no longer tenable. Indeed, the strategy seems to recognize as much, noting that "as a matter of principle, the United States will seek to exhaust all network defense and law enforcement options to mitigate any potential cyber risk to the U.S. homeland or U.S. interests before conducting a cyberspace operation."[6] Building the capability to carry out this mission is no small matter and should be the primary focus of the National Mission Forces.

For Cyber Command to use its offensive capability in defense of U.S. targets, it will need the ability to communicate securely and in real time with companies suffering attacks. In the event of a large-scale attack on the Internet, Internet routable communications could be down; moreover, if the attack involved the compromise of targeted systems, those systems might not be available and certainly would not be trusted to coordinate offensive action. Thus, for Cyber Command to play a role in defending the private sector, the government will need to extend a secure and classified communications network to Tier 1 Internet Service Providers, major information technology firms, and critical infrastructure companies. A model for such a network exists in the Defense Industrial Base Network (DIBnet), a secret-level classified network that the DoD provisions for communicating with Defense industrial base companies.[7] In line with the respective roles of the DoD and DHS, the role of provisioning the network should fall to DHS, with the DoD as one of many potential users.

The Digital Rubicon

The creation of DHS in 2002, after September 11, was an implicit recognition that even a catastrophic attack on American soil is not grounds for inviting the military into the domestic realm. In other areas parallel to cybersecurity, we can see why there is a role for a civilian agency in defending the homeland. Our borders are not patrolled by our military; that is the responsibility of the Border Patrol, a component of DHS. Likewise, the other civilian institutions that protect the American people within our borders are either contained within civilian federal agencies at DHS (the Coast Guard, the Transportation Security Administration, the Federal Emergency Management Agency [FEMA]) or the Department of Justice (FBI) or vested at the state and local level. Cybersecurity should be no different.

When civilian capacity fails, as FEMA did during Hurricane Katrina, DSCA may be an appropriate short-term response. As with that example, the appropriate long-term response is to build the necessary civilian capacity, not to make the military's role permanent. In the decade since Hurricane Katrina, FEMA has gone from being the most maligned federal agency to being the most well respected. In the most recent polling by Gallup, 75 percent of Americans are satisfied with federal response to disasters (note that in this same poll, homeland security efforts, at 57 percent, barely nudge out national defense, at 56 percent).[8] While DHS is not well-regarded in cybersecurity, the appropriate response is to build the capacity there, not to turn civilian mission over to the military.

As the DoD works to further refine its talking points on cyber warfare, it should strive to be clear that its role in defending the homeland in cyberspace is primarily in the use of offense to deter and disrupt malicious cyber activity. Network defense activity beyond the DoDIN is not and should not be the responsibility of the DoD. While DoD elements may provide support to private companies through DHS, this support should be limited, temporary, and no substitute for investments in cybersecurity by companies.

If the government judges that it must provide assistance to private companies, that assistance should be provided by DHS and its partner (civilian) sector-specific agencies. The mind-set that DHS should be a conduit whose authorities are used to channel DoD capability must end. The DoD has neither the scale to provide broad support to the private sector nor specialized capabilities that DHS could not acquire or that companies could not build or purchase on their own. If the next administration judges that government must intervene to provide protection to companies, it would be more effective and less cumbersome to simply subsidize cybersecurity for private companies rather than to attempt to provide security services.

Dating back to the Roman Republic, democracies have long held that the military's involvement in civilian life should be strictly limited. When Julius Caesar crossed the Rubicon River in 49 BCE and failed to turn over control of his legions to the ruling governor of the Italian province he entered, he violated that rule, setting into motion the events that would end the Republic. When President Obama issued a veto threat against the Cybersecurity Information Sharing Act in 2013 because it would allow direct sharing of information between the private sector and the NSA, it was in this vein of thinking.

> The Administration supports the longstanding tradition to treat the Internet and cyberspace as civilian spheres, while recognizing that the Nation's cybersecurity requires shared responsibility from individual users, private sector network owners and operators, and the appropriate collaboration of civilian, law enforcement, and national security entities in government.[9]

In short, the DoD must coordinate its role with the civilian agencies responsible for domestic security, not replace them. Its job is to conduct operations in cyberspace to blunt threats to the United States when network defenses are overwhelmed, not to operate those defenses. To do so would take our military service across the Digital Rubicon.

Notes

1. William J. Lynn III, "Defending a New Domain: The Pentagon's Cyberstrategy," *Foreign Affairs*, September–October 2010, https://www.foreignaffairs.com/articles/united-states/2010-09-01/defending-new-domain.
2. U.S. Government Accountability Office, "Information Security: DHS Needs to Enhance Capabilities, Improve Planning, and Support Greater Adoption of Its National Cybersecurity Protection System," January 2016, http://www.gao.gov/assets/680/674829.pdf.
3. U.S. Department of Homeland Security, "Enhanced Cybersecurity Services (ECS)," https://www.dhs.gov/enhanced-cybersecurity-services, accessed May 24, 2016.
4. Aliya Sternstein, "US Cyber Command Has Just Half the Staff It Needs," *Defense One*, February 8, 2015, http://www.defenseone.com/threats/2015/02/us-cyber-command-has-just-half-staff-it-needs/104847/.
5. Ellen Nakashima, "NSA Tries to Regain Industry's Trust to Work against Cyber-Threats," *New Haven Register*, October 11, 2013, http://www.nhregister.com/general-news/20131011/nsa-tries-to-regain-industrys-trust-to-work-against-cyber-threats.
6. U.S. Department of Defense, "The DoD Cyber Strategy," April 2015, http://www.defense.gov/Portals/1/features/2015/0415_cyber-strategy/Final_2015_DoD_CYBER_STRATEGY_for_web.pdf, 5.
7. DOD-DIB Cyber Incident Reporting and Cyber Threat Information Sharing Portal, http://dibnet.dod.mil/.
8. Jeffrey M. Jones and Steve Ander, "Americans Praise Gov't Work on Natural Disasters, Parks," *Gallup*, July 12, 2013, http://www.gallup.com/poll/163487/americans-praise-gov-work-natural-disasters-parks.aspx.
9. U.S. Office of Management and Budget, "Statement of Administration Policy, H.R. 624—Cyber Intelligence Sharing and Protection Act," April 16, 2013, https://www.whitehouse.gov/sites/default/files/omb/legislative/sap/113/saphr624r_20130416.pdf.

The U.S. Department of Defense Cyber Strategy

A Call to Action for Partnership

Michele Myauo

> As a matter of first principle, cybersecurity is a team effort within the U.S. federal government. To succeed in its missions, the Defense Department must operate in partnership with other departments and agencies, international allies and partners, state and local governments, and most important the private sector.
>
> U.S. Department of Defense (DoD) 2015 Cyber Strategy[1]

A call to action for partnerships with governments, academia, and industry is a key thread weaved throughout the DoD Cyber Strategy. The need for this "partnership" is cited over 50 times throughout the document.[2] Cybersecurity is a complex, rapidly evolving issue threatening global security and the economy. Mitigating cyber attacks requires the best and brightest minds globally working together to develop holistic approaches to mitigate cyber threats that impact security and the economy worldwide. This article provides an overview of the cyber-threat landscape and current U.S. government cybersecurity regulations and standards that set the context for the DoD Cyber Strategy. Three key areas of opportunity for governments, academia, and industry to partner with DoD to implement the strategy will then be discussed.

Cyber Threat Landscape

Cybersecurity is the ability to protect or defend an organization's IT environment against cyber attacks.[3] According to the IBM Cyber Security Intelligence Index, 2015 saw the greatest number of attacks originating (50 percent) and targeting assets in the United States (59 percent). Over 62 percent of incidents targeted just three industries: finance, insurance, and information and communications.[4] Cyber attackers are both internal and external to organizations, espousing a variety of motives ranging from financial, ideological, political, and combinations thereof. In 2015, 55 percent of malicious actors were persons with insider access to the organization's systems (31.5 percent malicious insiders, 23.5 percent inadvertent actor), and 45 percent were malicious outsiders.[5]

Threats internal to organizations include non-malicious, unintentional computer misuse and malicious, intentional corruption. An example of the latter was the incident at Saudi Aramco oil company. The insider cyber attacker initiated a virus that erased three-quarters of Aramco's corporate data, including documents, spreadsheets, e-mails, and other files, replacing the data with an image of a burning American flag.[6] Internal and external malicious actors are often motivated by financial and political considerations. Financially motivated criminal organizations engaged in cyber crime often target financial institutions, top executives, or high-value sensitive data that can be sold online for profit.[7]

Michele Myauo is a professor of engineering management and systems engineering at the George Washington University School of Engineering and Applied Science. She was previously director of cybersecurity at Microsoft and a service area manager and deputy director of enterprise architecture at IBM.

Ideologically and politically motivated cyber attacks are exemplified by such attacks as those conducted by hacktivists against the *New York Times* and the Stuxnet virus, the cyber warhead directed at an Iranian nuclear facility.[8] Nation-states can leverage politically and ideologically motivated hacktivists, cyberterrorists, and cyber militias to carry out cyber warfare, benefitting from the advantages of cyber attacks over traditional military attacks, such as the element of surprise, easy modification of attack techniques on short notice, and legal ambiguity due to lack of applicable international law covering cyber warfare that shields a nation from attribution and retribution.[9]

Cyber attacks by nation-states, cyberterrorists, and cyber militias are often targeted toward a particular entity. Cyber attackers gather information on the target from publicly available sources (also known as open source intelligence), analyze the information gathered, and reconstruct the target environment to plan the attack. The cyber attacker identifies the most vulnerable employees and networks and takes the path of least resistance. The cyber attacker then launches the attack against the target. The attack patterns vary, depending on information gathered and the environment.[10]

Overview of DoD Cyber Strategy

The DoD has the largest network in the world and relies on the Internet for mission-critical services. Its technological and military advantage is vulnerable to cyber attackers who work to disrupt and destroy networks and critical infrastructure and steal intellectual property. The purpose of the new DoD Cyber Strategy is to "guide the development of DoD's cyber forces and strengthen its cyber defense and cyber deterrence posture," focusing on building cyber capabilities and organizations for DoD's three cyber missions: defend DoD networks, systems, and information; defend the United States and its interests against cyber attacks of significant consequence; and provide integrated cyber capabilities to support military operations and contingency plans.[11]

The DoD Cyber Strategy sets five strategic goals and key implementation objectives to deter and mitigate cyber attack. They include the following:

§ Build and maintain ready forces and capabilities to conduct cyberspace operations
§ Defend the DoD information network, secure DoD data, and mitigate risks to DoD missions
§ Be prepared to defend the U.S. homeland and U.S. vital interests from disruptive or destructive cyber attacks of significant consequence
§ Build and maintain viable cyber options and plan to use those options to control conflict escalation and to shape the conflict environment at all stages
§ Build and maintain robust international alliances and partnerships to deter shared threats and increase international security and stability

The U.S. federal government has also reinforced the need to implement cybersecurity mitigations through federal law, more than 50 U.S. federal and state statutes address cybersecurity.[12] A brief overview of key cybersecurity doctrine and laws that complement the DoD Cyber Strategy is provided in the following paragraphs.

The 2002 Federal Information Security Management Act (FISMA) requires U.S. federal government agencies to assess their risks and implement appropriate security requirements and security controls tailored to meet organizational mission needs. The Federal Information Processing Standards (FIPS) are the U.S. government's minimum set of security controls for use in computer systems by nonmilitary U.S. government agencies and their contractors.[13]

In 2009 President Barack Obama created the Comprehensive National Cybersecurity Initiative to help secure U.S. assets in cyberspace.[14] In 2012 President Obama directed the DoD to defend the nation against cyber attack. In response, the DoD built the Cyber Mission Force, comprising over 6,200 military, civilian, and contractor personnel across the military and Defense Department to carry out DoD's cyber missions. In the 2013 Worldwide Threat Assessment, U.S. Director of National Intelligence James Clapper identified cyber threats as the number one threat to the United States.[15] The same year, President Obama signed Executive Order 13636, "Improving Critical Infrastructure Cybersecurity," to strengthen U.S. critical infrastructure against cyber attacks.[16]

According to Norse, a cybersecurity firm, 14 out of 22 federal agencies were not in compliance with FISMA, and there were 70,000 infosecurity issues at federal agencies in 2014, a 15 percent increase since 2013.[17] In 2014 other government regulations and standards were instituted to facilitate cybersecurity information sharing to include the Cybersecurity Information Sharing Act.[18] In the National Defense Authorization Act (NDAA) of 2014, Congress required the DoD to designate a principal cyber advisor to the secretary of defense to review and govern the development of DoD cyberspace policy and strategy.[19] The 2015 National Institute of Standards and Technology (NIST) Framework for Improving Critical Infrastructure Cybersecurity provides a comprehensive cybersecurity program structure for organizations to employ.[20] The framework addresses the need for enterprise architecture and incorporates technical and nontechnical (managerial) information-technology security standards from organizations, such as the International Organization for Standardization (ISO), the Institute of Electrical and Electronics Engineers (IEEE), the International Electrotechnical Commission (IEC), and NIST.[21]

Three Key Partnership Opportunities to Implement DoD Cyber Strategy

The DoD Cyber Strategy is a call to action for "partnership" with governments, academia, and industry, and the word "partnership" appears over fifty times throughout the document. With governments, academics, and industries worldwide working to mitigate the impacts of cyber attack, there are numerous opportunities for sharing tactics and techniques.

The DoD Cyber Strategy identifies the need for U.S. Cyber Command (USCYBERCOM) to outline requirements for building and maintaining a joint private- and public-sector workforce and capabilities to conduct cyberspace operations, including private-sector exchange programs throughout the design and development of new operational concepts. Private-sector actors, academia, and government agencies can work with USCYBERCOM to define and fulfill requirements for creating a joint training environment, including exercises and mission rehearsals, experimentation, certification, assessment, and development of cyber capabilities and tactics, techniques, and procedures for missions that cross boundaries and networks. The DoD will focus on ensuring its forces are prepared to operate using the capabilities and architectures they need to conduct cyber operations, while also building policy and legal frameworks to govern and integrate Cyber Mission Force employment into DoD's overall planning and force development. Three key areas of opportunity for government, academia, and industry to partner with DoD to implement the strategy are discussed here.[22]

1. Partnership Executing throughout the Cyber Systems Engineering Life Cycle

"DoD must be able to employ technical subject matter experts from the best cybersecurity and information technology companies in the country to perform unique engineering and analytic roles within DoD."[23] Systems engineering is an interdisciplinary approach that focuses on secure development and considers users' business and technical needs from project definition, development of concept of operations, architecture and requirements, system testing and verification, implementation, operations, and maintenance.[24] Partnerships in systems engineering initiatives across the cybersecurity life cycle are woven throughout the strategy. Cyber attacks exploit vulnerabilities in people, processes, and technologies; therefore, it is essential that systems engineers improve how cybersecurity is considered and addressed during the systems engineering life cycle, such as in enterprise architecture, to more effectively mitigate cyber attacks.[25]

Partnership with the private sector and academia in building the Joint Information Environment (JIE) single security enterprise architecture and information networks to meet the JIE's single security architecture is a key item addressed in the DoD Cyber Strategy. The single security architecture will adapt and evolve to mitigate cyber threats and will allow USCYBERCOM, combatant commands, and DoD components to maintain comprehensive situational awareness of network threats and secure the DoD enterprise in a unified manner. Fortunately, the U.S. government has reinforced the need for systems engineering artifacts, such as enterprise architectures, to support business decisions through federal law. The Clinger-Cohen Act of 1996 mandates that U.S. government agencies select and manage their IT resources by leveraging enterprise architectures, and the E-Government Act of 2002[26] requires the development of enterprise architecture to promote electronic government services.[27] The U.S. DoD Architecture Framework (DoDAF) is used by U.S. DoD agencies and communicates the enterprise architecture through a variety of architectural viewpoints.[28]

The DoD Cyber Strategy states the JIE's single security architecture will be developed with enhanced cyber situational awareness, deployed in response to validated requirements, and able to accommodate future defensive measures. The strategy outlines the need to strengthen the DoD information network, secure DoD data, and mitigate risks to DoD missions through strengthening the DoD's cybersecurity procurement and acquisition standards. This includes integrating cybersecurity standards into contracts for research, development, and procurement, as well as specifying additional cybersecurity standards for industry to meet. Given the U.S. government's historical focus on executing systems development and integration initiatives leveraging the systems engineering life cycle, academia and industry have responded with numerous educational institutions (including Carnegie Mellon, Georgetown University, the George Washington University, and the University of Maryland) and consulting firms (like Booz Allen Hamilton, IBM, Lockheed Martin, and Northup Grumman) stocked with systems engineering and cybersecurity professionals positioned to partner with the government. Furthermore, IT vendors across the infrastructure (such as Amazon, DellSecureWorks, Microsoft, Verizon Enterprise, and VMware) have invested in professional workforces focused on providing solutions for the federal government on premises, in the cloud, and in hybrid-cloud environments. Examples of secure services include Infrastructure as a Service (IaaS), Software as a Services (SaaS), and Platform as a Service (PaaS).

Outside assisting the development of DoD networks, academia and the private sector must work to secure defense-related data and harden U.S. networks and data against cyber attacks and cyber espionage. Many cyber attacks result from architectural debt within the organization and not leveraging secure development practices. By way of example, privilege escalation with credential theft via the Pass-the-Hash attack is identified by government, academia, and industries (e.g., the U.S. Computer Emergency Readiness Team, the SANS Institute, Microsoft, CyberArk) as one of the top cyber threats. In a Pass-the-Hash attack, the attacker targets workstations en masse via various means, including phishing e-mails. A phishing e-mail tricks a user into providing personal information or access to his/her computer network by impersonating a legitimate business. Once the unsuspecting user clicks on the e-mail, the user acting as the local administrator on the computer is compromised and the attacker harvests the user's credentials. The attacker can now impersonate said user. The attacker uses the credentials for lateral movement, including privilege escalation. Once the attacker acquires super user account status (e.g., "root" in Unix and Linux systems and "domain" in Windows-based systems), the attacker can exercise full control of data and systems in the environment to execute the attack mission (such as steal data, manipulate or destroy data and systems, etc.). Implementing a secure, tiered architecture for identity and access management mitigates this type of attack.[29]

2. Partnership Managing the Cyber Strategy and IT Portfolio

The DoD Cyber Strategy acknowledges the DoD must identify and plan the cybersecurity IT portfolio to defend the networks that support key DoD missions. In the face of cyber attacks, organizations must often make quick decisions with imperfect data. Given the opportunity for financial gain, social effect, and business impact, cyber-crime networks have evolved in sophistication.[30] Methods to capture necessary changes to the IT portfolio over time to meet these evolving cybersecurity needs are therefore essential.[31] Cybersecurity IT portfolio management involves balancing the performance of cybersecurity IT projects/programs with both risk and return on investments (e.g., CAPEX and OPEX), as it does for financial assets. It is important for nontechnical business managers and technical IT managers to collaborate early and often on IT portfolio management, as organizations must often balance the cost of security needs against competing priorities.[32]

Improving cyber budgetary management to transparently and effectively manage the DoD cyber operations budget is a key initiative of the DoD Cyber Strategy. To improve management of the cybersecurity IT portfolio, an intradepartmental team including the principal cyber advisor will work with DoD components through the Cyber Investment and Management Board (CIMB) to review DoD's cyber management. This includes developing DoD's cyber operations and cybersecurity policy framework consistent with presidential guidance. The DoD Cyber

Strategy also states the DoD will assess the cyber portfolio and establish the Joint Mission Assurance Assessment Program to assess and initiate the cybersecurity of current and future weapon systems.

Fortunately, the U.S. federal government has experience in, and has demonstrated the value of, utilizing private enterprise architecture frameworks to inform IT portfolio management and to fulfill mission needs. The Clinger-Cohen Act mandates twenty-seven U.S. federal government agencies to include the DoD to report their IT investment goals, costs, and statuses against the Federal Enterprise architecture (FEA).[33] The FEA provides a common taxonomy that enables stakeholders to communicate across organizational boundaries using a shared lexicon and supports business-based architecture analysis for government-wide improvement. Leveraging FEA IT investments across the U.S. government can be categorized and managed to streamline and optimize the entire IT portfolio.[34] Every year, the U.S. Office of Management and Budget (OMB) regulates the agency process for categorizing IT investments against the FEA in support of the budget appropriations processes.[35]

Academic researchers have also explored methods to manage cyber IT portfolios. For example, "An Expert Judgment Model to Assess Cyberattack Scenarios on Enterprise Architectures" proposes a rapidly deployable model that facilitates expression of cyber-attack scenarios via FEA to develop enterprise attack maps (EAMs) that describe cyber-attack scenarios using architectural language.[36] This model provides a common taxonomy that can be leveraged across the enterprise for swift architecture-based cybersecurity IT portfolio decision making.[37] In "A Macro Method for Measuring Economic-Benefit Returns on Cybersecurity Investments: The Table Top Approach," the authors recognize that methods are needed for capturing the changes in dynamic cybersecurity portfolios as technology and that cybersecurity adversaries enhance their capabilities over time.[38] Additionally, many government consulting firms, hardware, software, and cloud vendors, as well as traditional auditing firms (including Deloitte, EY, KPMG, and PricewaterhouseCoopers), are actively involved in assessing the government's maturity regarding their cyber mitigation posture.

3. Partnership Promoting Information Sharing to Facilitate Predictive Analytics

Cyber attackers share tactics, techniques, and procedures. In underground online cyber-crime communities, sellers post malware, attack tools, cyber-crime services, and stolen data (personal, corporate, etc.) for purchase.[39] Cyber attackers often target specific individuals, groups, or organizations, gathering information about the target from publicly available sources (i.e., open source intelligence) and launch attacks using a combination of open-source tools and social engineering tactics exploiting the most vulnerable aspects of infrastructure, the associated people, and their processes. Likewise, organizations across government, academia, and industry must band together and share information about cyber adversaries (e.g., motives, means, tactics, techniques) to better predict behaviors and implement effective cyber mitigations.

The DoD Cyber Strategy states private-sector actors must be prepared to defend the U.S. homeland and U.S. vital interests from disruptive and destructive cyber attacks of significant consequence. Collected data and metrics are the basis for actionable analysis to make business decisions supporting cyber-mitigation strategies and tactics. Open source data repositories, such as the National Vulnerability Database (NVD) and the Common Weakness Enumeration (CWE), are an excellent start to this information-sharing effort. The NVD is the publicly available U.S. government repository for the Security Content Automation Protocol (SCAP) methods for enabling automated vulnerability management, measurement, and policy compliance evaluation (e.g., FISMA compliance) and also contains several databases that are updated in near-real time to provide thousands of vulnerability notices, alerts, standards, and security measures. The CWE is an open source textual database of software vulnerabilities.[40]

Working together, the government and private sector can move beyond simply cataloging and counting vulnerabilities to more sophisticated predictive data analytics and machine learning. Some industry and academic institutes are already conducting such analysis. To make this possible, there is a need to gather and analyze cyber-attack data and patterns across government, academia, and industry. Continued research by government organizations (like NIST and US-CERT), academic institutes (such as Carnegie Mellon CERT and the SANS Institute), and commercial companies is needed to identify cyber signatures and potential cyber attacks before they occur. "We believe that data is the phenomenon of our time. It is the world's new natural resource. It is the new basis of competitive advantage, and it is transforming every profession and industry. If all of this is true—even inevitable—then cyber crime, by definition, is the greatest threat to every profession, every industry, every company in the world," Ginni Rometty, IBM chairman, president, and CEO, told CISOs (chief information security officers), CIOs, and CEOs from 123 companies in 24 industries at the 2015 IBM security summit.[41]

Conclusion

The DoD Cyber Strategy takes a holistic people, process, and technology approach to detecting and protecting against cyber attacks. Partnership among the DoD, government, academia, and industry within the three key areas of opportunity will accelerate implementation of the DoD Cyber Strategy and result in an increase in the overall resiliency of U.S. networks and systems.

Notes

1. U.S. Department of Defense, "The Department of Defense Cyber Strategy," April 2015, http://www.defense.gov/Portals/1/features/2015/0415_cyber-strategy/Final_2015_DoD_CYBER_STRATEGY_for_web.pdf.
2. Ibid.
3. National Institute of Standards and Technology (NIST), "Framework for Improving Critical Infrastructure Cybersecurity," February 12, 2014, https://www.nist.gov/document-3766.
4. "IBM 2015 Cyber Security Intelligence Index: Analysis of Cyberattack and Incident Data from IBM's Worldwide Security Services Operations," IBM research report, 2015, http://www-01.ibm.com/common/ssi/cgi-bin/ssialias?subtype=WH&infotype=SA&htmlfid=SEW03073USEN&attachment=SEW03073USEN.PDF.
5. Ibid.
6. Nicole Perlroth, "In Cyberattack on Saudi Firm, U.S. Sees Iran Firing Back," *New York Times*, October 23, 2012, http://www.nytimes.com/2012/10/24/business/global/cyberattack-on-saudi-oil-firm-disquiets-us.html?pagewanted=all&_r=0.
7. Kim-Kwang Raymond Choo, "Organised Crime Groups in Cyberspace: A Typology," *Trends in Organized Crime* 11, no. 3 (July

2008): 270–95, doi:10.1007/s12117-008-9038-9.
8. Ralph Langner, "Stuxnet: Dissecting a Cyberwarfare Weapon," *IEEE Security & Privacy* 9, no. 3 (May–June 2011): 49–51, doi:10.1109/MSP.2011.67.
9. Scott Applegate, "Cybermilitias and Political Hackers: Use of Irregular Forces in Cyberwarfare," *IEEE Security & Privacy* 9, no. 5 (September–October 2011): 16–22.
10. Aditya K. Sood and Richard Enbody, "Targeted Cyberattacks: A Superset of Advanced Persistent Threats," *IEEE Security & Privacy* 11, no. 1 (January 2013): 54–61.
11. Department of Defense, "Department of Defense Cyber Strategy."
12. Eric A. Fischer, "Federal Laws Relating to Cybersecurity: Discussion of Proposed Revisions," Congressional Research Service, April 23, 2012, https://www.law.upenn.edu/institutes/cerl/conferences/cyberwar/papers/reading/FederalLawsRelatingtoCybersecurity.pdf.
13. "Security and Privacy Controls for Federal Information Systems and Organizations: NIST Special Publication 800-53, Revision 4," National Institute of Standards and Technology, 2013, April 2013, doi:10.6028/NIST.SP.800-53r4.
14. "The Comprehensive National Cybersecurity Initiative," White House Office of the President, undated, https://www.whitehouse.gov/issues/foreign-policy/cybersecurity/national-initiative.
15. James R. Clapper, "Statement for the Record Worldwide Threat Assessment of the U.S. Intelligence Community, Senate Select Committee on Intelligence," February 9, 2016, https://www.dni.gov/files/documents/SASC_Unclassified_2016_ATA_SFR_FINAL.pdf.
16. "Executive Order: Improving Critical Infrastructure Cybersecurity," White House, Office of the Press Secretary, February 12, 2013, https://www.whitehouse.gov/the-press-office/2013/02/12/executive-order-improving-critical-infrastructure-cybersecurity.
17. See the Norse website, under "Markets" and "Government," http://www.norse-corp.com/markets/government/.
18. U.S. Congress, "S.2588—Cybersecurity Information Sharing Act of 2014," 113th Cong., https://www.congress.gov/bill/113th-congress/senate-bill/2588.
19. Department of Defense, "Department of Defense Cyber Strategy."
20. NIST, "Framework for Improving Critical Infrastructure Cybersecurity."
21. Ibid.
22. Department of Defense, "Department of Defense Cyber Strategy."
23. Ibid.
24. "What Is Systems Engineering?" International Council on Systems Engineering, undated, http://www.incose.org/practice/whatissystemseng.aspx.
25. Jennifer Bayuk and Ali Mostashari, "Measuring Systems Security," *Systems Engineering* 16, no. 1 (Spring 2013): 1–14. doi:10.1002/sys.21211.
26. "Guidance on Exhibits 53 and 300 Information Technology and E-Government," U.S. Office of Management & Budget, 2013, http://www.whitehouse.gov/sites/default/files/omb/assets/egov_docs/fy14_guidance_on_exhibits_53_and_300.pdf.
27. "The DoDAF Architecture Framework Version 2.02," Chief Information Officer, U.S. Department of Defense, August 2010, http://dodcio.defense.gov/Library/DoD-Architecture-Framework/.
28. Ibid.
29. "Mitigating Pass-the-Hash (PtH) Attacks and Other Credential Theft, Version 1 and 2," Microsoft, July 7, 2014, http://www.microsoft.com/en-us/download/details.aspx?id=36036.
30. Sood and Enbody, "Targeted Cyberattacks."
31. Paul R. Garvey, Richard A. Moynihan, and Les Servi, "A Macro Method for Measuring Economic-Benefit Returns on Cybersecurity Investments: The Table Top Approach," *Systems Engineering* 16, no. 3 (2012): 313–28, doi:10.1002/sys.21236.
32. Simon L. Garfinkel, "The Cybersecurity Risk." *Communications of the ACM* 55, no. 6 (2012): 29–32, doi:10.1145/2184319.2184330.
33. U.S. House of Representatives. Clinger Cohen Act of 1996, Pub. L. 104-106, divs. D, E,

Feb. 10, 1996, 110 Stat. 642, 679, available at Legal Information Institute, https://www.law.cornell.edu/topn/clinger-cohen_act_of_1996; see also "Clinger–Cohen Act," *Wikipedia*, accessed December 2014, http://en.wikipedia.org/wiki/Clinger%E2%80%93Cohen_Act.

34. "Guidance on Exhibits 53 and 300."
35. Ibid.
36. Michele Myauo, "Expert Judgment Model to Assess Cyberattack Scenarios on Enterprise Architectures" (PhD diss., George Washington University, 2016).
37. Ibid.
38. Garvey, Moynihan, and Servi, "Macro Method."
39. Choo, "Organised Crime Groups."
40. NIST, "National Vulnerability Database (NVD) Version," https://nvd.nist.gov/home.cfm.
41. Steve Morgan, "IBM's CEO on Hackers: 'Cyber Crime Is the Greatest Threat to Every Company in the World,'" *Forbes*, November 24, 2015; http://www.forbes.com/sites/stevemorgan/2015/11/24/ibms-ceo-on-hackers-cyber-crime-is-the-greatest-threat-to-every-company-in-the-world/.

Global Governance

What Happens If Cyber Norms Are Agreed To?

Emilio Iasiello

There is increased attention being placed on the potential establishment of nation-state "norms"—agreed-upon rules of behavior that will ideally reduce the possibilities of disproportionate response and conflict escalation—in cyberspace. Western interests, led by the United States, as well as China and Russia have visions of what such norms may look like, presenting their proposals before the United Nation's Group of Governmental Experts and the larger General Assembly, respectively. As more governments develop offensive cyber capabilities, there is a serious concern over the potential for online hostilities to escalate if states unknowingly overstep unannounced red lines. However, as most states have demonstrated a propensity to act in the interest of their own national security, the question remains—will cyber norms actually dissuade hostile cyber activity or just force it into more clandestine, sophisticated forms?

This article argues that cyber norms, even if universally enforced and accepted, may reduce the volume of easily detectable cyber espionage activity but will fail to address the more sophisticated activity that poses the greatest danger to high value targets. For the purposes of this article, it will be assumed that the terms and definitions have achieved acceptance and the agreed-upon behavior norms that will be implemented will likely include common principles expressed in the proposals to the UN. It will also assume that for those states having broken the established norms, sufficient and successful consequences exist to influence states not to overtly break them.

States Breaking Bad—The Call for a Code of Conduct

Over the past few years, governments have acknowledged possessing or developing offensive cyber capabilities. These countries include Australia,[1] China,[2] Denmark,[3] Iran,[4] South Korea,[5] the United States,[6] and the United Kingdom.[7] Such activities range from espionage to network reconnaissance to acts designed to disrupt, destroy, or manipulate information systems and the information resident on them. As more governments move toward developing offensive cyber capabilities, there is a recognized need to limit the potential fallout that can result from hostile cyber activities in order to preserve the stability and utility of the Internet. The calls for "cyber norms of behavior" are increasing, as states seek consensus on the lawful ways governments can and should use these new capabilities. Ideally, norms will reduce the risk of accidental or unintended conflict escalation.

While there have been efforts and recommendations made to establish these norms,

Emilio Iasiello has more than twelve years' experience as a strategic cyber intelligence analyst supporting U.S. government civilian and military intelligence organizations and a private-sector company providing cyber intelligence to Fortune 100 clients. He has delivered cyber threat presentations to domestic and international audiences and has published extensively in peer-reviewed journals.

particularly by international organizations such as the United Nations (UN), agreement has yet to be reached. Recent efforts include the following:

- In 2011 the United States put forth its ideas on how a nation-state should conduct itself in cyberspace in its *International Strategy for Cyberspace.*[8]
- Not to be outdone, China and Russia proposed their own code of conduct in September 2011,[9] and released an updated proposal in January 2015 that took into consideration edits and recommendations made by some of the member states of the United Nations.[10]
- In 2013, the Permanent Council of the Organization for Security and Co-operation in Europe issued a directive for OSCE member states to voluntarily implement confidence-building measures on the use and security of information and communication technologies (ICT), ensuring their consistency with international law, as well as the Helsinki Final Act.[11]
- In July 2015, the UN Group of Governmental Experts on Developments in the Field of Information and Telecommunications in the Context of International Security submitted its own set of recommendations to member states. The proposal advocated: states increase information sharing and assistance to prosecute terrorist and criminal acts committed using ICT; emphasize the promotion of human rights using ICT; refuse to knowingly support activity that intentionally damages or impairs critical infrastructure; and develop confidence-building measures to increase transparency, among other recommendations.[12]

Of particular note is that the countries most vocal about establishing a code of conduct are also the ones that are perceived to be the biggest purveyors of hostile online activity. While differences over definitions and interpretations remain between the U.S. and China/Russian positions, many of the same goals are expressed in both of the proposals, which suggests a consensus may not be far off. Critical security concerns, such as critical infrastructure protection, nation state coordination and cooperation, abstention from the use of ICT to engage in activity contrary to international peace and stability are consistently emphasized themes that would benefit all states. The establishment of such norms will undoubtedly help define an international consensus of "red lines"—in this case, the maximum level of accepted cyber malfeasance before a state will engage in punitive responses. Whereas the theft of intellectual property may provoke a certain level of response from the victim state, the deliberate denial, disruption, degradation, destruction, and/or manipulation of information systems or the information resident on them will likely receive a much stronger response. Given that the international community is seeking to achieve more multilateral control over how the Internet is run,[13] and the mounting frustrations over ongoing government-sponsored hostile cyber activities permeating the news on almost a daily basis,[14] a cyber code of conduct may be a closer possibility than previously thought.

However, would a code of conduct actually make a positive impact on the hostile activities it is supposed to reduce?

What Are Norms Supposed to Accomplish?

The term "cyber norms" refers to a more formalized process to regulate, or at least guide, nation-state conduct in cyberspace. The United States defines norms as "rules that promote order and peace, advance basic human dignity, and promote freedom in economic competition"; they should be grounded "in principles of responsible domestic governance, peaceful interstate conduct, and reliable network management."[15] Similarly, the China/Russia updated proposal promotes peace, security, openness, and cooperation, as well as "preventing the potential use of information and communication technologies for purposes inconsistent with the objectives of maintaining international stability and security."[16] The overlapping themes of both proposals are indicative of how consensus can be achieved, which is necessary to provide states an avenue for transparent engagement. Indeed, this sentiment is echoed by analysis by Royal United Services Institute, a UK organization dedicated to national security topics, that noted, "Non-adversarial and cooperative compliance processes that seek to facilitate compliance rather than punish noncompliance are more effective in encouraging changes of behavior."[17]

The majority of activity attributed to nation-states or their proxies is espionage,[18] including intellectual property theft[19] and network reconnaissance of key networks, particularly those of critical infrastructures.[20] There have been incidents that delivered disruption, such as distributed denial-of-service (DDoS) attacks;[21] destroyed information resident on systems;[22] and wreaked havoc on critical infrastructure components.[23] While these incidents have garnered considerable attention, they still represent only a small percentage of activity attributed to or suspected of being conducted by governments.

Attribution remains a challenging endeavor, despite public pronouncements made by some officials and security professionals to the contrary.[24] The Sony incident in particular highlights how "high confidence" has been given to North Korean culpability on the basis of technical indicators;[25] however, noted private cyber security experts disagreed on the government's findings, citing evidence that suggested complicit insiders or other foreign hackers played a role in the hack.[26] Public and private organizations use technical and threat analysis to track attacks and correlate information by classifying observed activity. Indicators of compromise; command and control (C&C) infrastructure; tactics, techniques, and procedures (TTP); and in some cases, a failure to maintain strict operational security procedures have all been leveraged for aggregation and attribution purposes. It follows that if nation-states agree to established norms of behavior based on mutually accepted principles of lawful conduct, they would likely have to adhere on some level to refraining from exploiting networks for intellectual property (IP) theft, espionage, or destructive acts, in order to evade proportionate political or economic repercussions.

But Nation States Do What Nation States Do

There is little doubt that states have a substantial interest in helping shape what an international cyber code of conduct entails to suit their own economic and national security concerns. States must demonstrate their commitment to being respectful partners in preserving peace and stability, while also engaging in above- and below-board activities that benefit their well-being. History is rife with examples of governments acting internationally in their own self-interest. The 2015 bombing of "terrorist" elements in Syria by the Russian Federation to strike at elements hostile to Russia's ally, the Syrian regime[27] and the 2003 U.S. invasion of Iraq to preempt the alleged development of weapons of mass destruction[28] are two recent examples of states pursuing unilateral national security objectives despite objection from the larger international community.

Cyberspace has enabled states to further these types of activities, now with reduced risk of exposure due to the anonymity afforded by the Internet and the inability of investigators to tie governments to an event owing to inadequate attribution measures. It follows that a nation-state will continue to use cyberspace to facilitate activities it deems within its interest to conduct, including espionage, IP theft, and in special circumstances, more destructive acts. Take the 2010 Stuxnet incident. The destruction of another state's critical infrastructure would generally be considered against the principles set forth by a cyber code of conduct. But if the aggressor (widely believed to be the orchestration of one or more collaborative governments) thought it was in its national security interest to use Stuxnet, it would likely have executed the attack regardless of its commitment to cyber norms or subsequent penalties that might have followed.

Ideally, cyber norms of conduct will empower the international community to levy proportionate responses for any infractions perpetrated by an offending state with sufficient consequences to deter future repeat violations from occurring. For norms to appear effective, nation-states must make the effort to comply with their dictates, as it would go against their international credibility for failing to do so. This just means the more sophisticated states (i.e., the ones currently spearheading cyber norm proposals) will have to actually make the effort to circumvent detection and identification measures or be more careful than current condition allows. In many instances when attribution is credibly established, such as the 2014 Sony incident[29] or the identification of a Chinese military unit behind a series of cyber intrusions,[30] operational security lapses provided the smoking guns for authorities to declare with sufficient confidence that they had identified the perpetrators. In light of these developments, coupled with other initiatives, such as the U.S. government's new cyber sanctions program, those wishing to still conduct operations in cyberspace will be forced to alter tactics, techniques, and procedures to further obfuscate their involvement. This may produce three unintended consequences:

- **Previously Tracked Activity Will Be Significantly Reduced**. One explanation as to why states, particularly those with reputed substantial cyber capabilities, continue to engage in overt and massive cyber espionage is that there has been little consequence to their actions. Public accusations,[31] indictments of military personnel,[32] and economic sanctions[33] have failed to deter even the most ardent cyber espionage states from curbing their activity or using more sophisticated methods when plausible deniability has sufficed to cast doubt. To maintain an upright public position after signing on to cyber norms, the volume of such activity will have be reduced to avoid tracking by public and private organizations. While on the surface, cyber norms will give off the illusion of having curbed hostile cyber activity, more sophisticated activities may be transpiring below the surface.
- **Previously Tracked TTPs Will Change**. Currently, private security vendors track several advanced persistent threat (APT) groups suspected of being nation-state or state-sponsored actors using a variety of technical analysis and TTPs that correlate to a group's activities. Once cyber norms are signed, states wanting to continue to leverage cyberspace for covert and clandestine purposes will have to burn all existing TTPs in favor of newer, more sophisticated and quieter alternatives. All known infrastructure, Internet protocol

addresses, malware, and methods of compromise would be changed considerably so no immediate connection could be made. The technical clues used in attribution analysis would only yield the type of information the attacker would want the defender to find. Tradecraft once perceived as sloppy could be tightened up or used in denial and deception techniques to execute cyber "sleight of hand." For example, the type of keyboard use and language in malware has been used to support attribution claims. However, if all the technical indicators pointed elsewhere (e.g., actors using different language keyboards, malware written in another language, infrastructure that points away from the sponsoring government), analysts could draw incorrect or misleading conclusions. According to Taia Global, the cyber security company's contacts in the Russian blackhat community revealed the Russian FSB regularly recruits hackers for contract work with the guidance they leave evidence pointing to an entirely different government as the attack's perpetrator.[34] Similarly, it would be prudent for all state actors to adopt similar strategies to evade attribution efforts.

- **Third-Country Operations Will Increase.** Even though most agree the last apparent source of an attack is not necessarily its actual origin, Internet protocol addresses and C&C infrastructure continue to be used as evidence to support attribution claims.[35] Even if hostile state-sponsored or state-directed actors previously operated within the supporting state's borders, under new norms this would likely stop. There is more opportunity and benefit for cyber operators to conduct their activities from third-party countries to further obfuscate attribution efforts. Furthermore, even if savvy defenders did track them down to a third-party country, if actions have been altered to manipulate technical indicators,[36] what type of fidelity can technical analysis truly provide?

Conclusion

While the news is rife with the suspected hacking activities China and North Korea, there is also reporting involving other countries engaged in offensive operations. Iran is suspected of conducting a cyber attack against Turkey causing a nationwide blackout for twelve hours.[37] Russian hackers have been identified as the culprits behind White House computer break-ins.[38] Lebanon is suspected of cyber espionage activity targeting several Middle East countries.[39] Attacks against worldwide supervisory control and data acquisition (SCADA) systems doubled in 2014;[40] many of these attacks involved APT actors, according to the U.S. ICS-CERT.[41] The need to establish cyber norms as a stabilizing force that can determine the parameters of acceptable conflict is understandable given the increase of destructive activities. However, if basic agreements can be reached, what does this mean for the majority of nondestructive activity currently transpiring across public and private sectors?

Currently, much of the APT-related activity has been characterized as persistent but lacking sophistication. Lack of effective consequences for these activities has generally not required these actors to use capabilities beyond what is necessary to exploit targeted systems or even employ strict OPSEC procedures. New norms may be the impetus for nation-states to increase their capabilities, substantially alter and implement newer TTPs not prone to immediate detection and monitoring, and improve OPSEC to include obfuscation as well as denial and deception. In essence, the security community would have to start from scratch in identifying perpetrators and tying them to responsible nation-state parties.

This is not to say there is not a role for cyber norms. Even the most basic rules can establish the necessary foundation for further international efforts, such as the creation of a global treaty limiting the scope and impact of hostile cyber activity. It is important governments trying to reach consensus keep in perspective the potential consequences that may result. By forcing known and observable cyber activity underground, the ability to monitor it under previous conventions is lost, potentially giving way to a more technically proficient and dangerous threat. Consideration needs to be paid for the next evolution of offensive cyber activity because one thing is for certain: it's not going away.

Notes

1. "Australian Defense Force Seeks to Develop Offensive Cyber Capabilities," *Tripwire*, May 8, 2014, http://www.tripwire.com/state-of-security/latest-security-news/australian-defense-force-seeks-to-develop-offensive-cyber-capabilities/.
2. "China Admits to Cyber Warfare Capabilities," *SC Magazine*, March 19, 2015, http://www.scmagazineuk.com/china-admits-cyber-warfare-capabilities/article/404478/.
3. Gerard O'Dwyer, "Denmark to Develop Offensive Cyber Capability," *Defense News*, January 8, 2015, http://www.defensenews.com/story/defense/policy-budget/cyber/2015/01/08/denmark-cyber-hackers-china-terma/21448705/.
4. "Iranian General: IRGC Cyber Warfare Capabilities Now Equal to Those of Major Global Powers," *Flash Critic*, January 4, 2014, http://flashcritic.com/iranian-general-irgc-cyber-war-capabilities-now-equal-those-of-major-world-powers/.
5. Zachary Keck, "South Korea Seeks Offensive Cyber Capabilities," *Diplomat*, October 11, 2014, http://thediplomat.com/2014/10/south-korea-seeks-offensive-cyber-capabilites/.
6. "U.S. Cyber Command Fact Sheet," Department of Defense, May 25, 2010, http://www.defense.gov/home/features/2010/0410_cybersec/docs/CYberFactSheet%20UPDATED%20replaces%20May%2021%20Fact%20Sheet.pdf (accessed April 24, 2015).
7. James Blitz, "UK Becomes First State to Admit to Offensive Cyber Attack Capability," *Financial Times*, September 29, 2013, https://www.ft.com/content/9ac6ede6-28fd-11e3-ab62-00144feab7de.
8. "International Strategy for Cyberspace," White House, May 2011, https://www.whitehouse.gov/sites/default/files/rss_viewer/international_strategy_for_cyberspace.pdf.
9. "Letter dated 12 September 2011 from the Permanent Representatives of China, the Russian Federation, Tajikistan and Uzbekistan to the United Nations addressed to the Secretary General," United Nations, A/66/359, September 14, 2011, https://ccdcoe.org/sites/default/files/documents/UN-110912-CodeOfConduct_0.pdf.
10. "Letter dated 9 January 2015 from the Permanent Representatives of China, Kazakhstan, Kyrgyzstan, the Russian Federation, Tajikistan and Uzbekistan to the United Nations addressed to the Secretary General," United Nations, A/69/723, January 13, 2015, https://ccdcoe.org/sites/default/files/documents/UN-150113-CodeOfConduct.pdf.
11. "Decision No. 1106: Initial Set of OSCE Confidence-Building Measures to Reduce the Risks of Conflict Stemming from the Use of Information and Communication Technologies," Organization for Security and Co-operation in Europe Permanent Council, PC.DEC/1106, December 3, 2013, http://www.osce.org/pc/109168?download=true.
12. "Group of Governmental Experts on Developments in the Field of Information and Telecommunications in the Context of International Security," United Nations, A/40/174, July 22, 2015, http://www.un.org/ga/search/view_doc.asp?symbol=A/70/174.
13. Ian Traynor, "Internet Governance Too U.S.-Centric, Says European Commission,"

Guardian, February 12, 2014, http://www.theguardian.com/technology/2014/feb/12/internet-governance-us-european-commission.

14. "World Leaders React to NSA Spying Reports," *USA Today*, October 29, 2013, http://www.usatoday.com/story/news/world/2013/10/29/nsa-spying-merkel-hollande-cameron-reaction-obama/3294343/; Katy Barnato, "China Accused of Decade of Cyber Espionage in Asia," CNBC, April 13, 2015, http://www.cnbc.com/id/102580878.
15. "International Strategy for Cyberspace."
16. "An International Code of Conduct for Information Security—China's Perspective on Building a Peaceful, Secure, Open, and Cooperative Cyberspace," United Nations Institute for Disarmament Research, February 10, 2014, http://www.unidir.ch/files/conferences/pdfs/a-cyber-code-of-conduct-the-best-vehicle-for-progress-en-1-963.pdf.
17. Mark Phillips, Jennifer Cole, and Jennifer Towers, "Cyber Norms of Behavior," RUSI, https://www.rusi.org/downloads/assets/Cyber_norms_of_behaviour_report_-_Executive_Summary.pdf.
18. Kelly Jackson Higgins, "Nation-State Cyber Espionage Targeted Attacks Becoming Global Norm," *Dark Reading*, February 10, 2015, http://www.darkreading.com/attacks-breaches/nation-state-cyber-espionage-targeted-attacks-becoming-global-norm/d/d-id/1319025.
19. Mike Walls, "Nation-State Cyberthreats: Why They Hack," *Dark Reading*, January 8, 2015, http://www.darkreading.com/informationweek-home/nation-state-cyberthreats-why-they-hack-/a/d-id/1318522.
20. David E. Sanger and Nicole Perlroth, "Iran Is Raising Sophistication and Frequency of Cyberattacks, Study Says," *New York Times*, April 15, 2015, http://www.nytimes.com/2015/04/16/world/middleeast/iran-is-raising-sophistication-and-frequency-of-cyberattacks-study-says.html?_r=0.
21. Eneken Tikk, Kadri Kaska, and Liis Vihul, "International Cyber Incidents: Legal Considerations," Cooperative Cyber Defence Centre of Excellence, 2010, https://ccdcoe.org/publications/books/legalconsiderations.pdf.
22. Danielle Walker, "Analysis of Wiper Malware, Implicated in Sony Breach, Exposes Shamoon-Style Attacks," *SC Magazine*, December 4, 2014, http://www.scmagazine.com/analysis-of-wiper-malware-implicated-in-sony-breach-exposes-shamoon-style-attacks/article/386781/.
23. David E. Sanger, "Obama Order Sped Up Wave of Cyberattacks against Iran," *New York Times*, June 1, 2012, http://www.nytimes.com/2012/06/01/world/middleeast/obama-ordered-wave-of-cyberattacks-against-iran.html.
24. Jeffrey Carr, "Responsible Attribution: A Prerequisite for Accountability," NATO Cooperative Cyber Defence Centre of Excellence, Tallinn Paper No. 6 (2014), https://ccdcoe.org/sites/default/files/multimedia/pdf/Tallinn%20Paper%20No%20%206%20Carr.pdf.
25. Kim Zetter, "Critics Say New Evidence Linking North Korea to the Sony Hack Is Still Flimsy," *Wired*, January 8, 2015, http://www.wired.com/2015/01/critics-say-new-north-korea-evidence-sony-still-flimsy/.
26. Jeff Goldman, "Researchers: Sony Hack was Insider Breach," *eSecurity Planet*, December 31, 2014. http://www.esecurityplanet.com/network-security/researchers-say-sony-hack-was-insider-breach.html.
27. Holly Yan and Melissa Gray, "Putin: Russian Airstrikes in Syria Aimed at Helping al-Assad Regime," CNN, October 12, 2015, http://www.cnn.com/2015/10/12/world/syria-russia-airstrikes/.
28. Elizabeth Wishnick, "Strategic Consequences of the Iraq War: U.S. Security Interests in Central Asia Reassessed," Strategic Studies Institute, May 2004, http://www.strategicstudiesinstitute.army.mil/pdffiles/PUB383.pdf.
29. Brian Donohue, "FBI Officially Blames North Korea," *Threat Post*, December 19, 2014, https://threatpost.com/fbi-officially-blames-north-korea-in-sony-hacks/109999/.
30. "APT 1: Exposing One of China's Cyber

Espionage Units," Mandiant, 2013, https://www.fireeye.com/content/dam/fireeye-www/services/pdfs/mandiant-apt1-report.pdf.

31. Cory Bennett, "Obama Calls Out China for Cyber Espionage," *The Hill*, February 6, 2015, http://thehill.com/policy/cybersecurity/231998-obama-security-plan-highlights-chinese-cyber-espionage.
32. Ellen Nakashima, "Indictment of PLA Hackers Is Part of Broad U.S. Strategy to Curb Chinese Cyberspying," *Washington Post*, May 22, 2014, http://www.washingtonpost.com/world/national-security/indictment-of-pla-hackers-is-part-of-broad-us-strategy-to-curb-chinese-cyberspying/2014/05/22/a66cf26a-e1b4-11e3-9743-bb9b59cde7b9_story.html.
33. Matt Schiavenza, "Why North Korea Sanctions Are Unlikely to Be Effective," *Atlantic*, January 3, 2015, http://www.theatlantic.com/international/archive/2015/01/why-north-korea-sanctions-are-unlikely-to-be-effective/384188/.
34. Jeffrey Carr, "Cyber Threat Intelligence: More Threat than Intelligence?" *Digital Dao Blog*, March 30, 2015, http://jeffreycarr.blogspot.com/2015/03/cyber-threat-intelligence-more-threat.html.
35. "APT 1"; "Putter Panda," CrowdStrike, http://cdn0.vox-cdn.com/assets/4589853/crowdstrike-intelligence-report-putter-panda.original.pdf.
36. Carr, "Cyber Threat Intelligence."
37. Robert Morley, "Iran Accused of Massive Cyberattack on Turkey," *Trumpet*, April 29, 2015, http://www.thetrumpet.com/article/12583.19.0.0/world/terrorism/iran-accused-of-massive-cyber-attack-on-turkey.
38. Evan Perez, "How the U.S. Thinks Russians Hacked the White House," CNN, April 8, 2015, http://www.cnn.com/2015/04/07/politics/how-russians-hacked-the-wh/.
39. Kelly Jackson Higgins, "Lebanon Believed to Be Behind Newly Uncovered Cyber Espionage Operation," *Dark Reading*, March 31, 2015, http://www.darkreading.com/attacks-breaches/lebanon-believed-behind-newly-uncovered-cyber-espionage-operation/d/d-id/1319695.
40. Mike Lennon, "Attacks against SCADA Systems Doubled in 2014: Dell," *Security Week*, April 13, 2015, http://www.securityweek.com/attacks-against-scada-systems-doubled-2014-dell.
41. "Incident Response and Vulnerability Coordination in 2014," *ICS CERT Monitor*, US ICS-CERT, September 2014–February 2015, https://ics-cert.us-cert.gov/sites/default/files/Monitors/ICS-CERT_Monitor_Sep2014-Feb2015.pdf.

Dysfunction, Incentives, and Trade

Rehabilitating U.S.-China Cyber Relations

Rebecca Liao

U.S.-China cyber relations, which had been festering since technological exchanges between the two countries began in the 1990s, came to a head in 2013. After four years of bilateral talks hinting at the importance of cybersecurity, U.S. and Chinese policymakers finally began discussions to enact formal rules of conduct. Both the United States and China highlighted the urgency of the problem. Vice President Joe Biden asked China to end the "outright" theft of intellectual property,[1] while National Security Advisor Tom Donilon said that Chinese cyber attacks are "not solely a national security concern or a concern of the U.S. government" but also amount to "sophisticated, targeted theft of confidential business information and proprietary technologies."[2] Indeed, credible evidence suggests that actors with direct links to the Chinese government had been hacking the computer systems of both American companies and the U.S. government, stealing commercial and military secrets.[3] Later that year, Beijing had a ready rejoinder: Edward Snowden revealed that U.S. cyber espionage by the National Security Agency (NSA) was far more extensive than previously believed.[4]

If current U.S-China cybersecurity tensions had an accelerant, it was Operation Aurora, in which groups with ties to China's People's Liberation Army hacked several major U.S. technology companies, including Google, Adobe Systems, Yahoo, and Symantec. These attacks took place over the latter half of 2009 and were first reported by Google in 2010. Aside from the breadth of attacks, what was most significant was that the hackers had stolen proprietary source code, a company's most valuable and closely guarded intellectual property.[5] In 2013 the U.S. cybersecurity firm Mandiant published a report alleging that People's Liberation Army Unit 61398, based just outside Shanghai, was responsible for the persistent theft of U.S. company trade secrets and other data.[6] A 2014 report by the Center for Strategic and International Studies estimated that the U.S. economy loses approximately $100 billion each year from cyber espionage and other cyber crimes.[7] Losses that can be traced back to China have yet to be quantified, though American stakeholders ranging from state manufacturers associations to the National Bureau of Asian Research have estimated that they are significant.[8]

For its own part, the United States has extensively hacked Huawei Technologies, China's largest telecommunications company, to find security vulnerabilities in the country's networks.[9] The Snowden leaks further revealed that the NSA had tapped Chinese communications through the Chinese University of Hong Kong.[10] Though directed by a government agency, these cyber activities were made possible only through the aid of U.S. Internet companies, including the use of "metadata and technical design information to exploitation of technical control

Rebecca Liao is director of business development at Globality Inc., a stealth startup in Silicon Valley. She is also a writer and China analyst. Her writing has appeared in the *New York Times*, *Financial Times*, *Foreign Affairs*, the *Atlantic*, and the *National Interest*, among other publications.

points in cloud computing infrastructure located on U.S. soil," according to cybersecurity expert Jon Lindsay.[11] As a result, China has accelerated its efforts to become less dependent on U.S. technology companies. Apple, Cisco, Google, IBM, Intel, Microsoft, Oracle, and Qualcomm all saw sales in China fall significantly in the aftermath of the Snowden revelations.[12] Recently, China has focused its protective efforts on its banking system. Draft bank regulations released in early 2015 required that foreign companies selling equipment to Chinese banks disclose their source code. The regulations were tabled because of European and American protest, but the technology and data access requirements for foreign companies have resurfaced in a counterterrorism law.[13]

Dysfunctional Relations

Despite both countries' willingness to establish a cybersecurity pact, no enforceable solutions have presented themselves. The U.S.-China Cybersecurity Working Group, begun in 2013, came to a screeching halt in May 2014 when China withdrew. Earlier that month, U.S. prosecutors had brought charges against five Chinese military officers for cyber theft.[14] Around the same time, according to an EY survey of German companies, "the U.S. now poses almost as big a risk as China when it comes to industrial espionage and data theft."[15] At the culmination of Chinese president Xi Jinping's visit to the United States in September 2015, he and President Obama announced an agreement between the two countries to abstain from cyber espionage in the commercial arena.[16] Comprising broad outlines and pledges, the pact was more of a symbolic gesture than a concrete step toward establishing a bilateral cybersecurity regime. Shortly afterward, Crowdstrike Inc., a U.S. software security company, reported that five U.S. technology companies and two pharmaceutical companies had been hacked by Chinese sources.[17]

In other parts of the world, cybersecurity agreements have been just as difficult to implement. The Council of Europe's Convention on Cybercrime, ratified by forty states (including the United States) in 2001, enacted several measures to solve the problem of attribution in cyber crimes. Because of the widespread availability of malware and other covert techniques, plausible deniability is a ready defense for any accused party. The convention created additional measures requiring official state agencies to refrain from cyber attacks, punishing the countries from which cyber attacks originate, encouraging countries to share information with one another about potential bad actors, and standardizing domestic cyber security measures across states.[18] But because they were not backed up by enforcement mechanisms and relied too heavily on collective policing, these solutions have proved ineffective.

Evidenced by continued cyber attacks against one another by the two states, U.S.-China cyber relations suffer from the same fundamental problems. Neither party has the ability to police the other, and both have much to gain in terms of technological advantage and competitive espionage. In addition, China—along with Russia and other members of the Shanghai Cooperation Organization—has aggressively pushed for the international community to recognize "Internet sovereignty," each country's ability to set its own Internet protocols and regulations.[19] At the World Internet Conference in 2015, President Xi advocated this policy by stating the global community should "respect the right of individual countries to choose their own path to cyber development, model of cyber regulation and participate on the same footing."[20] Coupled with a counterterrorism law enacted in late 2015 that requires foreign companies to provide technical assistance to China's counterterror efforts, Beijing's ask becomes clear. China will accept the idea of international cooperation on cybersecurity, but only on its own terms.

Applying Game Theory to U.S.-China Cyber Relations

The problem is that neither China nor the United States has had, on balance, any incentive to stick to an agreement on cyber activity: both currently benefit more by exploiting one another. How can we design an enforceable agreement for this situation? One solution lies in the theory of exploitative games.

U.S.-China cyber relations can be modeled as the classic Prisoner's Dilemma game: While it is most beneficial for both states to cooperate with one another rather than "defect" from any potential agreement by not cooperating, the most rational response to either state's decision is to defect. As long as the rational strategy for both states is to defect, both will end up with suboptimal payoffs. But the game changes if it is played multiple times—that is, if it is played iteratively—because the states have a chance to learn each other's strategies over time and respond accordingly. As Robert Axelrod first established by conducting vast trials of Iterated Prisoner's Dilemma (IPD) games, the optimal strategy for both players is tit for tat.[21] In other words, each player should play in the next round as the opponent had played in the previous. In 2012 William Press and Freeman Dyson revealed that for IPD games in which at least one player is able to exploit the other, this strategy is no longer optimal.

In exploitative games, one or both players can "(i) deterministically set her opponent's score, independently of his strategy or response or (ii) enforce an extortionate linear relation between her and his scores."[22] A strategy that satisfies both of these conditions is known as a zero-determinant strategy. One common example of such a strategy is unilateral defection in a one-shot Prisoner's Dilemma game: No matter what strategy the one player employs, it is best for the other to defect since there are no future rounds to reward cooperation.

The simplest way to understand the consequences of a zero-determinant strategy is to simulate games in which it is played while varying the characteristics of the players. Namely, the IPD game assumes players are of two types: sentient and evolutionary. The former has a theory of mind about the opponent; the latter has no such theory and is merely reactive to the opponent's moves.

We assume that Player X has a zero-determinant strategy but Player Y does not. If X believes Y has no theory of mind about her, then X may freely exploit Y, and the best that Y can do is to cooperate with X rather than defect. If, however, X believes Y may have a theory of mind about her, then X will watch Y's behavior over multiple rounds to confirm and, in doing so, determine that the best strategy is to employ a zero-determinant strategy that will afford Y fairer payoffs. Now, assuming both players have a zero-determinant strategy, should neither player be sentient, both would play their exploitative strategies and yield low payoffs all around. If both are sentient, then their best strategy after a few rounds of extortion is to negotiate a cooperative equilibrium. Both should agree to unilaterally set the other's payoffs to what that player would receive in this equilibrium. That way, neither player can benefit by violating the treaty between them, and both are punished for further exploitative behavior.[23]

How might this IPD game apply to U.S.-China cyber relations? China's zero-determinant strategy was largely laid out in the 2006 National Medium to Long-Term Plan (MLP) for the Development of Science and Technology. The primary policy of the MLP is the promotion of "indigenous innovation" across a comprehensive swath of industries. This will be achieved by converting foreign technology for domestic use through a four-part process: introduce, digest, assimilate, and re-innovate.[24] The introduction of foreign technology can be accomplished through several means: joint ventures, partnerships, open source intelligence, knowledge from Chinese nationals abroad, and of course, espionage.

Advanced persistent threats (APTs), or cyber attacks, from China focus on U.S. government and military agencies, as well as industries that Beijing is particularly interested in fostering. In addition, APTs collect data on Chinese dissidents and Asian international institutions. From 2005 to 2013, there were thirty-seven cases of alleged APTs from China, the most famous being the penetration of Google and other major U.S. technology companies. In 2010, around the time Beijing implemented the MLP, the main targets of APTs shifted from government and defense contractors to commercial entities.[25] The coincidence has led many international technology companies to consider the MLP "to be a blueprint for technology theft on a scale the world has never seen before."[26] Given a fifteen-year time frame for implementation and the capital- and time-intensive process of adaptation and innovation, it is no surprise that espionage became a principal strategy of the plan.

Following the Snowden revelations, China has introduced another dimension to its cyber strategy. Foreign technology companies must hand over their source code and locate servers hosting user data on Chinese soil. Beijing justifies these demands by invoking national security concerns, but the United States believes such posturing to be a cover to get technology companies to hand over their trade secrets directly.[27]

Meanwhile, the United States' zero-determinant strategy is much more focused on traditional espionage. The NSA's penetration of Chinese telecommunications companies is focused on gaining access to the communications of Chinese officials, not stealing technology. Similarly, the United States has its own analogue to China's protectionist measures against foreign technology companies: the Committee on Foreign Investment in the United States (CFIUS), a notoriously opaque regulatory body that examines all major foreign investments, including all acquisitions, made in the United States. If a transaction is found to pose a national security threat, then the deal will not be allowed. The vast majority of deals, including milestone technology deals in sensitive sectors such as semiconductors, are approved.[28] However, this proportion is skewed since the shadow of CFIUS informs these transactions from the beginning stages of their negotiation. Many proposed deals, including Tsinghua Unigroup's potential acquisition of Micron Technology, were scuttled after being deemed unlikely to pass CFIUS review.[29] The committee's particular focus on China has drawn allegations of distinct bias against Chinese companies and investors in U.S. cross-border deals. Even the purchase of the American-owned Smithfield Foods by China's Shuanghui International, a merger of food conglomerates, underwent an extensive CFIUS process despite being unrelated to matters of national security.[30]

So far, the United States and China have pursued their strategies unilaterally without regard to the other's behavior. This has led to the current outcome: An equilibrium of low payoffs consisting of national security vulnerabilities, stolen trade secrets, and technology protectionism. Both nations are sentient about the other's strategy, so the best solution is to agree to the cooperative equilibrium and severely punish any defection. The most successful area of cooperation thus far between the two countries has been in the economic realm. But what would an economic solution for U.S.-China cyber relations entail?

The Centrality of Trade

The international community has dealt with cybersecurity as a fundamental issue of trade. Historically, multilateral and bilateral trade agreements (BITs) were the main protection for foreign companies' trade secrets.[31] Given the growing problem of cyber breaches, a new family of agreements has emerged to address the issues directly. Finalized in 2015, the Trans-Pacific Partnership (TPP) bars member countries from requiring foreign software companies to hand over their source code.[32] Importantly, however, the TPP does not include China. In the meantime, Beijing is seeking to use its considerable economic resources and relationships with its Asian neighbors as leverage to reap the benefits of joining the TPP without actually becoming a member state.[33] The U.S.–European Union (EU) trade negotiations have sought to address extensive NSA surveillance of EU targets. Finally, the World Trade Organization (WTO) has enforcement mechanisms at its disposal for cyber attacks that may be employed if they are not a threat to national security.[34] Whether any of these mechanisms will successfully delineate and implement a robust cybersecurity regime remains to be seen.

Meanwhile, the private sector has made significant headway. U.S.-China tech partnerships boomed in 2015 after a cooling-off period stemming from China's uncertain economy, bureaucratic red tape, and lack of protection for intellectual property.[35] China's appetite for the latest innovations and advanced technological infrastructure is at full throttle. Chinese tech companies are also accelerating investments in their U.S. counterparts in exchange for a platform to distribute and market to Chinese consumers.[36] Early in 2015, Baidu, China's largest search engine, and Uber reached an agreement whereby Baidu would integrate its maps app, the most popular in China, with the Chinese Uber app. The fruits of that partnership are now manifesting in Uber's rapid expansion across Chinese cities.[37] Baidu also inked a deal with CloudFlare Inc., a U.S. Internet security company, to provide its products across seventeen of Baidu's data centers. Recognizing that it would have to play by China's controversial Internet security protocols, CloudFlare assured its customers that none of their data would pass through its China network unless expressly authorized.[38]

The compromises CloudFlare devised to ensure smooth entry into the China market are becoming increasingly common after nearly two decades of a high failure rate for U.S.-China joint ventures.[39] Dell has gone so far as to announce a $125 billion "In China, for China" campaign. To date, Dell's new strategy has yielded deals to help a state-owned enterprise develop high-performance servers and to partner with Kingsoft, a Chinese software company, to create a cloud product. Importantly, both of Dell's projects involve bolstering a national security interest for China.[40]

Domestic technological security in China was also a player in a recent flurry of semiconductor deals. Intel made a $1.5 billion investment in Tsinghua Unigroup, China's largest chip developer.[41] Hewlett Packard sold 51 percent of its China networking gear unit to them as well.[42] Qualcomm has agreed to license its 3G and 4G wireless technologies to two Chinese smartphone makers, Beijing Tianyu Communication Equipment Co. and the Haier Group.[43] Echoing Dell, IBM announced its "Made with China" initiative in early 2015, through which it will work with multiple Chinese companies to build the country's advanced chip industry.[44]

Perhaps the most surprising of these deals is the last one: IBM had been hard hit by China's shift to a more protectionist technology policy. In response to the U.S. cyber espionage activities exposed by the Snowden leaks, China dropped several U.S. tech companies as providers—including IBM, Cisco, Apple, and Intel—because their products were deemed to be a cybersecurity threat. [45] For U.S. companies, frustrations still linger over the Chinese government's general preference for domestic companies and the lack of transparency and efficiency in the regulatory regime.[46]

Most significantly, these tech deals reflect a slight but important shift in focus from one-way technology transfer and joint development to a more even exchange of access to products and services. For example, Cisco announced that it had formed a joint venture with Inspur, a Chinese server manufacturer, to distribute networking and cloud computing products in China.[47] Didi Kuaidi, Uber's rival in China, is set to partner with LinkedIn on artificial intelligence, further buttressing LinkedIn's already successful venture into China.[48] In the aftermath of President Xi Jinping's visit to Seattle in 2015, Microsoft was the biggest winner of all: inking deals to make Baidu the default search engine on Windows 10 in China and to sell cloud computing services by 21Vianet Group, a Microsoft-backed Chinese company, to state-owned enterprises.[49] While none of these partnerships is guaranteed to work, they indicate a path toward a cooperative equilibrium between the United States and China on cyber relations.

Judging by the volume and severity of complaints U.S. and Chinese technology companies have had in the past about poor cyber relations, their business ventures cannot be expected to carry the day without significant support from a formal trade regime. Only by pledging to reward each other for good behavior and punish bad behavior, and by engaging the technology sector to make this agreement a reality, can the United States and China move forward on cyber relations.

For China, this would entail curbing its cyber espionage and allowing U.S. technology companies to enter the country with fewer market restrictions and burdensome requirements to share technology or grant access to trade secrets. These terms could be incorporated into the expansive BIT that the United States and China are currently negotiating. A revised "negative list" of industries in which U.S. entities cannot freely invest or set up shop in China is part of this agreement and should include fewer technology sectors.[50] And while the protection of source code should remain non-negotiable, the United States ought to allow for some flexibility in technology sharing. Given China's seriousness about the MLP, U.S. companies will continue to be de facto compelled to transfer intellectual property or risk having it stolen by Chinese hackers incentivized to do so. A much more practical outcome would allow for technology sharing, but if and only if China reciprocates.

In return, the United States should make the CFIUS process more transparent and efficient. The process is currently a virtual black box that can extend for months after a transaction is formally agreed to, leading to Chinese complaints that it is unfair and constitutes latent discrimination.[51] What CFIUS should do instead is maintain regular communication with the parties to the transaction and make available nonclassified documentation associated with the case. Beijing has gone a step further and asked that China be granted "most-favored-nation" status under CFIUS review, such that transactions involving its companies will not be subject to higher scrutiny than that imposed on other countries' companies.[52] While this request appears fair, it is impossible to implement in practice since each country with which CFIUS deals presents different national security challenges.

These concessions should be made with the understanding that if cyber theft is detected, they will be suspended until the proper international body processes the claim of cyber theft and renders judgment. The specific dispute resolution mechanism can closely mirror that of the WTO, which has proved to be effective so far in resolving conflicts that are both time sensitive and time-consuming to investigate.

Conclusion

Current approaches to U.S.-China cyber relations focus on designing sufficient disincentives for bad behavior. Given the mutually exploitative nature of U.S.-China cyber relations so far, this is a suboptimal strategy for both parties. A sustainable enforcement regime must include accretive benefits to cooperation as well. For technology sectors as economically interdependent as those between the United States and China, a cybersecurity regime can be complete only if it includes and encourages greater trade and investment between the two countries' technology sectors.

Notes

1. "Biden: China Must Stop 'Outright' Theft of U.S. Trade Secrets," *Voice of America*, July 11, 2013, http://www.voanews.com/content/biden-china-must-stop-outright-theft-of-us-trade-secrets/1699447.html.
2. Tom Donilon, "The United States and the Asia-Pacific in 2013" (speech at the Asia Society, New York, March 11, 2013), https://www.whitehouse.gov/the-press-office/2013/03/11/remarks-tom-donilon-national-security-advisor-president-united-states-an.
3. David E. Sanger, David Barboza, and Nicole Perlroth, "Chinese Army Unit Is Seen as Tied to Hacking against U.S.," *New York Times*, February 18, 2013.
4. James Griffiths, "Two Years after Snowden, NSA Revelations Still Hurting U.S. Tech Firms in China: Report," *South China Morning Post*, July 3, 2015.
5. Ariana Eunjung Cha and Ellen Nakashima, "Google China Cyberattack Part of Vast Espionage Campaign, Experts Say," *Washington Post*, January 14, 2010.
6. "APT 1: Exposing One of China's Cyber Espionage Units," Mandiant, 2013, https://www.fireeye.com/content/dam/fireeye-www/services/pdfs/mandiant-apt1-report.pdf.
7. "Net Losses: Estimating the Global Cost of Cybercrime" (Washington DC: Center for Strategic and International Studies, 2014).
8. "Chinese Cyber Theft Presents Massive Problem for U.S. Economy," *Bulletin*, http://www.pamanufacturers.org/pma-bulletin/chinese-cyber-theft-presents-massive-problem-us-economy; and "The IP Commission Report: The Report of the Commission on the Theft of American Intellectual Property" (Washington, DC: National Bureau of Asian Research, 2013).
9. David E. Sanger and Nicole Perlroth, "NSA Breached Chinese Servers Seen as Security Threat," *New York Times*, March 22, 2014.
10. Tom Phillips, "Edward Snowden Claims U.S. Hacks Chinese Targets," *Telegraph*, June 13, 2013.
11. Jon R. Lindsay, "The Impact of China on Cybersecurity: Fiction and Friction," *International Security* 39, no. 3 (Winter 2014–15): 7–47.
12. Ibid.
13. Gillian Wong, "U.S. Presses China on Technology Rules," *Wall Street Journal*, February 27, 2015.
14. Ting Shi and Michael Riley, "China Halts

Cybersecurity Cooperation after U.S. Spying Charges," *Bloomberg*, May 20, 2014, http://www.bloomberg.com/news/articles/2014-05-20/china-suspends-cybersecurity-cooperation-with-u-s-after-charges.
15. Chris Bryant, "NSA Claims Put German Business on Guard," *Financial Times*, November 1, 2013.
16. Julie Hirschfeld Davis and David E. Sanger, "Obama and Xi Jinping of China Agree to Steps on Cybertheft," *New York Times*, September 25, 2015.
17. Joseph Menn, "China Tried to Hack U.S. Firms Even after Cyber Pact: CrowdStrike," October 19, 2015, http://www.reuters.com/article/us-usa-china-cybersecurity-idUSKCN0SD0AT20151020.
18. Jack Goldsmith, "Cybersecurity Treaties: A Skeptical View" (Stanford, CA: Hoover Institution, 2011).
19. Alex Grigsby, "Will China and Russia's Updated Code of Conduct Get More Traction in a Post-Snowden Era?" (New York: Council on Foreign Relations, 2015).
20. James Griffiths, "Chinese President Xi Jinping: Hands off Our Internet," CNN, December 16, 2015, http://www.cnn.com/2015/12/15/asia/wuzhen-china-internet-xi-jinping/.
21. Robert Axelrod, *The Evolution of Cooperation* (New York: Basic Books, 2006).
22. William Press and Freeman Dyson, "Iterated Prisoner's Dilemma Contains Strategies That Dominate Any Evolutionary Opponent," *Proceedings of the National Academy of Sciences of the United States of America* 109, no. 26 (2012): 10409–13.
23. See ibid; and Alexander Stewart and Joshua Plotkin, "Extortion and Cooperation in the Prisoner's Dilemma," *Proceedings of the National Academy of Sciences of the United States of America* 109, no. 26 (2012): 10134–35.
24. James McGregor, "China's Drive for 'Indigenous Innovation:' A Web of Industrial Policies" (Washington, DC: U.S. Chamber of Commerce, 2010).
25. Lindsay, "Impact of China on Cybersecurity."
26. McGregor, "China's Drive."
27. Tom Mitchell, "China Approves Controversial Antiterrorism Law," *Financial Times*, December 27, 2015.
28. Theodore Moran, "Chinese Investment and CFIUS: Time for an Updated (and Revised) Perspective" (Washington, DC: Peterson Institute for International Economics, 2015).
29. Liz Hoffman and William Mauldin, "Micron Shares Jump on Tsinghua Bid Despite Expected U.S. Regulatory Scrutiny," *Wall Street Journal*, July 14, 2015.
30. Shruti Date Singh and Bradley Olson, "Smithfield Receives U.S. Approval for Biggest Chinese Takeover," *Bloomberg*, September 6, 2013, http://www.bloomberg.com/news/articles/2013-09-06/smithfield-receives-u-s-regulator-approval-for-shuanghui-deal.
31. Scott J. Shackelford, Eric L. Richards, Anjanette H. Raymond, and Amanda N. Craig, "Using BITs to Protect Bytes: Promoting Cyber Peace by Safeguarding Trade Secrets through Bilateral Investment Treaties," *American Business Law Journal* 52, no. 1 (2015): 1–74.
32. "Summary of the Trans-Pacific Partnership Agreement," Office of the United States Trade Representative, October 4, 2015.
33. Andrea Chen, "It's Not Checkmate Yet: Beijing to Counter U.S.-Led Trans-Pacific Partnership Trade Pact," *South China Morning Post*, October 7, 2015.
34. Shackelford et al., "Using BITs to Protect Bytes."
35. "Price of Admission: A Timeline of U.S. Tech Companies' Recent China Deals," *Wall Street Journal*, September 14, 2015.
36. Thilo Hanemann and Daniel H. Rosen, "High Tech: The Next Wave of Chinese Investment in America" (New York: Asia Society, 2014).
37. Ingrid Lunden, "Uber Has Raised $1.2B More in China with Baidu Investing as Rival Didi Kuaidi Gets $3B," *Techcrunch*, September 7, 2015, http://techcrunch.com/2015/09/07/uber-confirms-its-raised-1-2b-more-in-china-led-by-baidu-as-rival-didi-kuaidi-gets-3b/.
38. Paul Mozur, "Baidu and CloudFlare Boost Users over China's Great Firewall," *New York Times*, September 13, 2015.

39. Stephan Bosshart, Thomas Luedi, and Emma Wang, "Past Lessons for China's New Joint Ventures," McKinsey & Company, December 2010, http://www.mckinsey.com/insights/corporate_finance/past_lessons_for_chinas_new_joint_ventures.
40. "Dell Says to Invest $125 Billion in China over Five Years," *Reuters*, September 10, 2015, http://www.reuters.com/article/us-dell-china-idUSKCN0RA0G920150910.
41. "Intel and Tsinghua Unigroup Collaborate to Accelerate Development and Adoption of Intel-Based Mobile Devices," Intel Corporation, September 25, 2014, http://newsroom.intel.com/community/intel_newsroom/blog/2014/09/25/intel-and-tsinghua-unigroup-collaborate-to-accelerate-development-and-adoption-of-intel-based-mobile-devices.
42. Tony Robinson, "HP Sells Control of China Units for $2.3 Billion to Tsinghua," *Bloomberg*, May 21, 2015, http://www.bloomberg.com/news/articles/2015-05-21/hp-says-tsinghua-holdings-to-buy-control-of-chinese-asset.
43. Don Clark and Anne Steele, "Qualcomm Reaches License Deals with China's Tianyu and Haier," *Wall Street Journal*, December 29, 2015.
44. "Cisco Joins Flurry of U.S.-China Tech Partnerships," *Reuters*, September 24, 2015, http://www.reuters.com/article/us-cisco-systems-china-idUSKCN0RO0AE20150924.
45. Matthew Miller, "Spy Scandal Weighs on U.S. Tech Firms in China, Cisco Takes Hit," *Reuters*, November 14, 2013, http://www.reuters.com/article/us-china-cisco-idUSBRE9AD0J420131114.
46. McGregor, "China's Drive."
47. "Cisco Joins Flurry of U.S.-China Tech Partnerships."
48. Ingrid Lunden, "LinkedIn and Uber's China Rival Didi Kuaidi Ink Deal to Partner on Apps, R&D and Recruitment," *Techcrunch*, September 23, 2015, http://techcrunch.com/2015/09/23/linkedin-and-ubers-china-rival-didi-kuaidi-ink-deal-to-partner-on-apps-rd-and-recruitment/.
49. Robert McMillan and Gillian Wong, "Microsoft Forms New Partnerships in China," *Wall Street Journal*, September 24, 2015.
50. Annie Lowrey, "U.S. and China to Discuss Investment Treaty, but Cybersecurity Is a Concern," *New York Times*, July 11, 2013.
51. Moran, "Chinese Investment and CFIUS."
52. Ibid.

International Cyber Norms Dialogue as an Exercise of Normative Power

Eneken Tikk-Ringas

> To have power is to be taken into account in others' acts [policies].
>
> —Harold D. Lasswell and Abraham Kaplan, *Power and Society: A Framework for Political Inquiry*

The fourth session of the United Nations Group of Governmental Experts (UN GGE) on International Information Security concluded with an excellent testament of the interaction between law and politics.[1] Leaving legal positivists frustrated with the lack of progress in restating seemingly obvious international legal provisions, the report of the experts offers a treasure chest for analysis of how great cyber powers make use of norms as an instrument of power.[2]

The intersection of law, policy, and strategy in the international cybersecurity dialogue is at the core of this inquiry, putting special emphasis on the systematic and structured use of normative instruments in support of national interests pertaining to the development and use of information and communication technologies (ICTs). Evident in this dialogue are competing narratives on the benefits and threats embedded in widespread uses of ICTs as views derive from diverging priorities and evidence a gulf of capacity and capabilities.

The increasingly structured and systematic use of normative instruments in support of national interests invites attention to the normative strategies of leading cyber powers. Aspirations to shape legal thought target the current balance of power and speak to diverging visions of what *ought to be*. Norms, as technology itself, serve calculated and purposeful aspirations to shape the perception of the "new normal" that Manners refers to as the greatest power of all.[3] In Wolfers's terms, states are up to shaping the milieu in which they are going to operate.[4] Given the diametrically different visions of "open, resilient, stable, secure and peaceful cyberspace," materializing such visions requires global subscription to what is to become the leading narrative.

The discourse of normative power has been extensively developed under the "normative power Europe" agenda. Manners and Tocci[5] derive their normative power framework from Carr's distinctions among economic power, military power, and power over opinion;[6] Duchêne's *idée force*;[7] and Galtung's "ideological power as the power of ideas."[8] Diez aligns EU normative power with hegemony, implicitly recognizes the power-interest nexus within normative power, yet stays loyal to the established European Union discourse Manners has set.[9]

This article deliberately decouples the discourse of normative power from the liberalist-ethical considerations attached to it in the "normative power Europe" discourse.[10] Leaving aside handles of "unprecedented political forms," "no gain," and overly loaded terms such as "hegemony,"

Eneken Tikk-Ringas is the consulting senior fellow for the Future Conflict and Cyber Security Programme at the International Institute for Strategic Studies. She previously worked as legal advisor and led the legal and policy team at the NATO Cooperative Cyber Defence Centre of Excellence in Tallinn, Estonia.

this article views the exercise of normative power as the use, by states, of normative instruments for shaping *how things ought to be within the normative space*. This approach helps to observe what states are making of international law, thereby adding dimensions to the discussion of the development of international law, both in the context of international cybersecurity specifically and technological advances more broadly.

Examination of the UN GGE as an exercise of state power follows the discourse of "normative power," constellated in the first part of the article. The author then turns to reviewing the progress made in the three consecutive GGEs, mapping the outcomes of this process to the positions of the three leading powers—the United States, China, and Russia. The article discusses the potential of the UN GGE as a normative tool and platform for countries to further promote their national interests related to development and uses of ICTs. Finally, the article will draw from these discourses some recommendations on adding the dimension of normative power in the exercise and analysis of modern statecraft.

Normative Power

The following is a contribution to what Berenskoetter refers to as the "third dimension" of power: shaping normality.[11] It builds on Keohane's and Nye's analysis of international rules, norms, and procedures as an intervening factor in the interdependence of states.[12] It acknowledges the relationship between national interests and norms, addressed by Finnemore.[13] It treats norms as an objective of state interests of its own right. It furthers Finnemore's and Sikkink's analysis on how norms come to being and how they create political change by emphasizing how states push for standards of behavior to achieve their goals.[14]

Normative power, therefore, is about serving national interests by normative instruments and, by Rosecrance, "setting world standards in normative terms."[15] It features Therborn's "telling other parts of the world what political, economic and social institutions they should have."[16] It also includes what Manners refers to "normalizing" rules and values in international affairs through noncoercive means, with the intention to redefine "normal" in international relations.[17]

At the core of normative power is the goal of attracting others to join in one's vision of what the "norm" is. Attached to it is a calculated and purposeful aspiration to influence the world order by shaping the normative conscience of the international community. Underlying this agenda is the idea of the *civilizing* potential of treaties, rules, and norms. Viewing international law as providing justifications to relatively new international cybersecurity issues invites and allows (re-)determining applicable norms, (re-)offering own interpretations, and suggesting new norms to be adopted as a baseline of law's objectivity.[18]

The normative space goes beyond the "internal" and "external" distinction as bilateral, multilateral (including regional and subregional), and universal aspirations can be identified in the interest areas of states acting as norm entrepreneurs[19] or norm externalizers.[20] However, especially in the context of globalization and the increasing technology dependence of world affairs, the milieu in which nations seek to operate is global.[21]

Normative frameworks provide a grid for legitimating and illegitimating the exercise of state power. At the time when violence and force of arms are replaced with the "more gentle constraint of uninterrupted visibility,"[22] legal checks and balances of low-profile power projection become subject to extra scrutiny. Therefore, open issues on "norms" are far from trivial. National positions on the legal status of norms, modalities of their application, and further development are elementarily attached to more fundamental aspirations and, especially in the context of ICTs, to widely differing national capacity and capabilities.

"Cyber" is, of course, not the first or the only arena where the emergence and utility of normative power can be witnessed. Case studies in Tocci's comparison of the EU normative power posture to those of the United States, Russia, India, and China offer a variety of examples,[23] as does Ingebritsen's take on Scandinavia's role in world politics.[24] Furthermore, the emergence of "rules or rule-complexes, legal institutions and spheres of legal practice" (referred to as fragmentation of international law)[25] and the so-called regime complex[26] can be seen as functions of the growing normative interests, inputs and outputs in international politics.

Changes in international affairs are enabling, if not inviting, the emergence of normative power. As the sensitivity to disruption and disturbances has increased, existing legal frameworks and thinking dating to the era of great wars and survival do not necessarily match the expectations of today. As a result, international law no longer offers a refuge for states, itself becoming an arena of great power ambitions and contestation. Resulting from this are openings for restating international law and the existing normative concepts in new, previously uncontested contexts.

Normative instruments of power can serve other instruments of state power—military, economic, informational, and technological. The quest for cyber norms ranges from the considerations of development and uses of military cyber capabilities to broader issues of trust and confidence in the information society the same technologies helped build and sustain. The convergence of computing and communication technologies changes the nature of government and accelerates the diffusion of power.[27]

It is essential to remember the weight attached to norms, and especially international law, in the eyes of some key actors. Chinese contemporary international legal thought views the international legal order seeded by Grotius, Vattel, and the Peace of Westphalia as a tool to sustain Western dominance.[28] The United States' entry into the formation of international law in the late nineteenth century added to the instrumental view of international law in great politics. This reality highlights the interrelationship between world politics and the development of both domestic and international norms.

Norms

"Normative" is to be regarded broadly for the purposes of examining the nexus between norms and state interests. Following Merriam-Webster, normative refers to what is (to be) considered to be the usual or correct way of doing something.

The pursuit of norms does not stop at legally binding "hard norms." While there are strong views among legal scholars about the existence and value of "soft law," relevant norms play an increasingly prominent role in contemporary international relations and their influence is likely to increase in the future.[29] It is therefore necessary to address issues that attach to the ambivalence in the concept of the norm.

A comprehensive normative approach acknowledges international law's many origins but expands the scope of accepted and appropriate mechanisms to soft law and other legally nonbinding instruments. This broadened approach is outlined later, and comes from Terpan, who argues for soft law's impact in both legally binding and nonbinding norms.[30]

Applying a broad approach to rules and normative instruments corresponds to the emerging understanding of feasible and functional remedies. For example, were studies of general principles of law or national and corporate approaches to reveal significantly diverging practices, this would signal for a possible call for unification of views in those areas. Should examination of domestic practices evidence predominant unity in any given question, that unity as a common nominator could be usefully turned into the next international consensus development platform and utilized as treaty or custom base. Were one to discover countries lack any substantially new views on matters, this would seriously indicate no need for new law. In line with this, where countries cannot agree on modalities of implementation of international law, nonbinding norms, rules, and principles offer a parallel track.

UN GGE as an Exercise of Normative Power

The UN GGE is instrumental to the UN-level discussions of the threats to international information security. While perhaps not the Hague Peace Conferences for cybersecurity, the UN GGE is the venue for addressing the future of norms in the context of advances in ICTs.[31] First proposed by the Russian Federation in 2001, the group of governmental experts was first established in 2004 to help the UN secretary-general "consider existing and potential threats in the sphere of information security and possible cooperative measures to address them" and to conduct a study "on international concepts aimed at strengthening the security of global information and telecommunications systems."[32]

Four GGEs have convened since 2004. The first GGE (2004/2005) did not produce a consensus report. The second GGE (2009/2010), called to "continue to study existing and potential threats in the sphere of information security and possible cooperative measures to address them," recommended steps for confidence-building and other measures to reduce the risk of misperception over ICT disruptions.[33] In particular, the second GGE invited further dialogue among states to discuss norms pertaining to state use of ICTs and to reduce collective risk and protect critical national and international infrastructure and recommended confidence-building, stability, and risk-reduction measures to address the implications of state use of ICTs.[34]

The third GGE (2012/2013) continued the discussion of confidence-building measures and broadened the discussion on norms, rules, and principles of responsible behavior by states into two separate threads: applicability of international law and norms of responsible state behavior. Accordingly, the 2014/2015 GGE report addressed norms, rules, and principles for the responsible behavior of states (chapter 3) separately from how international law applies to the use of ICTs (chapter 6), framing the former as "voluntary, non-binding norms" that do not seek to limit or prohibit action that is otherwise consistent with international law.[35]

The three leading themes of the UN GGE are closely related and often difficult to distinguish in practice. In their essence, international law, nonbinding norms of behavior and CBMs are all normative instruments. However, following the reasoning of the group, the norms discussion is aimed at further developing voluntary mechanisms that turn into measurable and verifiable actions once implemented.

The tripartite agenda of the UN GGE embraced a critical review of existing international law, potential areas of norms development, and concrete short-term remedies against the most urgent cyber threats. Thus, the GGE operates within the broadest margins of "the normative," understood as standards of behavior, obligations, responsibilities, rights, and duties of states.

While the first GGE failed to produce a consensus report, it was an important milestone in growing Russian normative power. When the United States and other like-minded states refused to discuss international law in the context of ICTs, Russia still found a way to shape international cyber behavior. Russian success demonstrates the equalizing power of the UN, where, in an expert-level working group, Russia is on par with the United States, discussing matters of technological development when its own leadership and cyber capabilities are modest.

Of many standards of behavior under discussion at the UN GGE, three merit special attention owing to their intertwinement with conflicting state interests. These are the applicability of international humanitarian law (IHL) to conflict in cyberspace, the free flow of information, and state responsibility for malicious and hostile activities in cyberspace.

1. The Applicability of International Humanitarian Law

Washington used the 2015 GGE to confirm existing principles of international law serve as the appropriate framework to identify and analyze rules and norms of behavior that should govern the use of cyberspace. Although the report does not mention the Law of Armed Conflict (LOAC), it contains language referring to the inherent right of self-defence under Article 51 of the UN Charter and affirms the IHL principles of humanity, necessity, proportionality, and distinction.

The United States refuses to accept any restriction on current norms of LOAC. U.S. policy seeks to dissuade and deter malicious actors, making clear Washington reserves the right to defend its vital national assets as deemed necessary and appropriate.[36] The uncertainty from the lack of consensus would be anxiety inducing for the country with uncontestably superior cyber capabilities. The integrity of existing international law, including LOAC, supports the U.S. stand for a broader culture of responsibility and accountability to sustain stability online as well as off. Protecting civilian targets is a core U.S. security policy objective, and LOAC provides guarantees against assault the United States perceives herself most targeted and vulnerable to.[37]

That the GGE affirmed the applicability of LOAC in cyberspace confirms this issue was not settled in the previous GGE (although emphasized by the United States as one of the key outcomes of the 2013 GGE).[38] For Russia and China, there is little loss in meeting the West in its aspirations to prove LOAC is a useful legal regime to deal with cyber issues. Failure to compromise could have meant normative defeat with no advancements at all. Moreover, the Chinese objective—cyberspace as peaceful space—is underscored in the same paragraph from which the applicability of LOAC is inferred. The report prominently highlights the principles of sovereign equality, the settlement of international disputes by peaceful means, obligation to refrain from threat or use of force, and nonintervention in internal affairs that all flow from the Sino-Russo language. In particular, China and Russia have joined forces to promote an alternative norms agenda in the UN. The Code of Conduct on International Information Security forwards Sino-Russo interpretations of international law.

2. Free Flow of Information

One of the main disagreements between states is the condition of free flow of information. The GGEs have been unable to make progress on the issue of human rights, where the US anchored its freedom of information plea. The status quo, whereby Washington reads Article 19 of the ICCPR as consisting of two paragraphs,[39] while Moscow focuses on the third, illustrates the gulf between the two camps.[40] This perfect normative problem,however, will hardly lend itself to resolution.[41] The U.S. position since signing the ICCPR in 1992 is that states party to the covenant should wherever possible refrain from imposing any restrictions or limitations on the exercise of the rights recognized and protected by the covenant, even when such restrictions and limitations are permissible under the terms of the covenant.[42] For the United States, this statement follows from the First Amendment in force since 1791.[43] In contrast, Russia frequently compares ICTs to weapons of mass destruction and views decentralized and uncontrolled information flows dangerous to internal stability. The "information security" doctrine emphasizes information as part, if not the core, of the problem.

Deliberations at the GGE merge into the broader issue of Internet governance. Russia has called for a state-centric model of Internet governance, whereas the United States is advocating for a decentralized "multistakeholder model." The split between these two camps became evident in the 2012 vote on International Telecommunication Regulations, where, 89–55, a significant minority, voted against ITU's (and therefore a government-centric) approach to Internet governance.[44] The United States protested the explicit inclusion of Internet and Internet governance in the treaty, as well as ITU's claim of authority in cybersecurity.[45]

More broadly, both freedom of information and the issue of Internet governance flow into the question of national sovereignty in cyberspace. When it comes to the fundamental principle of sovereignty, there is little doubt of its applicability, as the very exercise of the UN GGE negotiations testifies to countries' making use of their statehood. However, the modalities of exercise of national sovereignty depend on what will be the accepted protection area of "freedom of information" and "privacy" or who ends up making decisions about the administration of the Internet infrastructure. This contextualizes the Sino-Russo position that respect for freedoms in information space are subject to restrictions provided by (national) law.[46]

3. Rhetoric of Responsibility

Another semitransparent normative agenda in the UN GGE is that of accountability. From the U.S. perspective, the question is both about responsibilities of states in assuring cybersecurity and about deterrence against asymmetric attacks. Ability to defend against cybersecurity threats would reduce the likelihood of malicious activities routed through the "responsible actors'" territories, reduce the load on law enforcement, and result in trust and confidence that supports both economic growth and social stability.

These instruments socialize the U.S. position that effective cybersecurity is not merely a matter of government or law enforcement practices but must be addressed through prevention and supported throughout society. For the United States, the discourse of norms at the UN GGE is another vehicle for promoting its long-standing efforts to "advance norms for individual and State behavior in the interest of cybersecurity."[47] The 2015 GGE cemented the global culture of cybersecurity, a 2001 U.S. initiative.

As expected, states were not in unanimous agreement on the premises and extent of state responsibility, a legal concept with contested status.[48] Experts decided to note the accusations of organizing and implementing wrongful acts brought against states should be substantiated.[49] Commenting on the issue, the Russian expert explained,

> The charges of the organization and implementation of cyber attacks must be proven. This eliminates the possibility of indiscriminately holding a state responsible for the attack it had allegedly committed in the information space, as it was in the case of the sanctions which the United States introduced against North Korea in response to hacking the servers of the film company Sony Pictures.[50]

State responsibility clauses have also been inserted into the chapter of (nonbinding) norms, rules, and principles rather than international law.[51] What follows from this practice is the conclusion that State consensus is absent on the scope and essence of these normative constructs at this time. This leads back to the "bottom lines" of the current discourse.

Considerations of Normative Power beyond GGE

States' determination to use norms to support their international aspirations goes well beyond the GGE. "Stability through norms" is a chapter in the U.S. international cybersecurity strategy.[52] Then–State Department legal advisor Koh explained, "Compliance with international law frees us to do more, and do more legitimately, in cyberspace, in a way that more fully promotes our national interests."[53] The White House has publicly promoted international regulatory cooperation as reducing, eliminating, or preventing unnecessary differences in regulatory requirements.[54]

On the other hand, the United States has maintained for years that countries need to improve their ability to categorize and remedy malicious and hostile uses of ICTs. For a legally strategic and cognizant country, the authority of the international legal order creates a level of predictability and stability. A law-abiding international community would mean more responsible state behavior and predefined ramifications for operations in and through cyberspace—where the United States enjoys a dominant role.

Normative arguments have become a tool for the reformulation of Russia's messages to the world, while being embedded in Russia's understanding of its international power. Makarychev argues President Putin is not only eager to get involved in the global norms debate but tries to use it to reassert Russia's leadership.[55] Referring to a set of norms Russia considers universally accepted deprives Russia of any responsibility for their articulation. In addition, Putin accepts the responsibility of transforming and adapting these norms to support universal applicability.[56]

During the fifteen-year GGE process, Russia has remained skeptical about the efficacy of international law in cyberspace, taking the view that not all legal norms "automatically" extend to interstate relations in the field of ICTs and relevant criteria need to be specified.[57] Moscow's signature on the GGE reports has not made it change its position on the need to adapt international law to ICTs. Such a position is logical for an underdog in the technological race but also consistent with the Kremlin's ambition to keep the world alert of the military potential of ICTs. Russia and China have reason to distrust the U.S. use of cyber capabilities owing to Washington's military superiority and considerable expertise in operating in the cyber domain and the global Internet.

Other governments and organizations have taken up the role of norms in pursuit of their cybersecurity interests. Kenya sees "increased incentives to participate in the formation of international rules" as one of benefits of improved cybersecurity.[58] An Estonian GGE expert, addressing the European Dialogue on Internet Governance, echoed the conclusion of the 2013 GGE, adding, "We have all agreed that international law applies to the cyber sphere. . . . We do not need new international treaties, but rather a consensus on how existing international law applies to cyberspace."[59]

The Global Conference on Cyberspace (GCCS) Chairman's Statement stressed the need for broad and inclusive engagement to enhance shared understandings of how international law applies to state activities in cyberspace. In particular, the statement pointed out that the ability of states to settle their international disputes peacefully would benefit from shared understandings of what might constitute a threat or use of force in cyberspace for the purposes of Article 2 (4) of the UN Charter.[60] Similarly, the Asian-African Legal Consultative Organization conference, running parallel to the GCCS, examined "how the existing norms of IHL apply, and whether there is a need for new rules or principles in order to comprehensively address cyber warfare."[61]

Conclusion

Countries don't just promote their interpretations of existing international law; they also utilize nonbinding norms to shape new expectations of behavior. They are pushing new normality and making use of regimes as an instrument of their normative aspirations, using both bilateral and multilateral platforms to support the international norms agenda.

The exercise of normative power by states merits closer analysis, as it will help develop narratives that socialize one's own normative aspirations and dissolve undesired normative initiatives. It is essential to apply academic research and analysis to normative strategies of states, as this will support identifying potential allies and consensus camps for norm entrepreneurship.

After all, positions tabled at the UN GGE and other international venues are not simply legal positions, they are declarations of fundamental values and interests states are determined to guard and promote. As such, these positions reflect more than "state understanding of international law"—they reflect the potential and future of international law, as the latter can only be what states make of it. This emphasizes the value of "soft" norms designed to overcome acute issues or a temporary lack of codified international legal consensus. At the same time, the effort that states put into making clear their dissent regarding existing international norms demonstrates their determination to keep international law "flexible enough." One should therefore not expect quick solutions to difficult cybersecurity questions.

Notes

1. The UN GGE was first called for in 2001 under the Russia-sponsored series of resolutions on Developments in the Field of Information and Telecommunications in the Context of International Security. Since 2004 the GGE has met four times. The 2014/2015 GGE report was the third report to examine existing and potential threats arising from the use of ICTs by states, as well as possible measures to limit such threats. United Nations Office for Disarmament, "Fact Sheet: Developments in the Field of Information and Telecommunications in the Context of International Security," July 2015, https://unoda-web.s3.amazonaws.com/wp-content/uploads/2015/07/Information-Security-Fact-Sheet-July2015.pdf.
2. UN Secretary-General and UN Group of

Governmental Experts on Developments in the Field of Information and Telecommunications in the Context of International Security, *Group of Governmental Experts on Developments in the Field of Information and Telecommunications in the Context of International Security: note / by the Secretary-General (A/70/174)* (New York: United Nations, July 22, 2015), http://www.un.org/en/ga/search/view_doc.asp?symbol=A/70/174.

3. Ian Manners, "Normative Power Europe: A Contradiction in Terms?" *Journal of Common Market Studies* 70, no. 2 (2002): 253.
4. Arnold Wolfers, "The Goals of Foreign Policy," in *Discord and Collaboration: Essays on International Politics* (Baltimore: Johns Hopkins University Press, 1962), 67–80.
5. Manners, "Normative Power Europe"; and Nathalie Tocci, ed., *Who Is a Normative Foreign Policy Actor? The European Union and Its Global Partners* (Brussels: Centre for European Policy Studies, 2008).
6. Edward Hallett Carr, *The Twenty Years' Crisis 1919–1939: An Introduction to the Study of International Relations* (London: Macmillan, 1962), 108.
7. François Duchêne, "The European Community and the Uncertainties of Interdependence," in *A Nation Writ Large? Foreign Policy Problems before the European Community*, ed. Max Kohnstamm and Wolfgang Hager (Basingstoke, UK: Macmillan, 1973), 2 and 7.
8. Johan Galtung, *The European Community: A Superpower in the Making* (London: Allen & Unwin, 1973), 33.
9. Thomas Diez, "Normative Power as Hegemony," *Cooperation and Conflict* 48, no. 2 (2013): 194–210.
10. At the same time not dismissing Condliffe: "Power, involving the possible use of force, is not necessarily evil but may be used to achieve moral purposes." J. B. Condliffe, "Economic Power as an Instrument of National Policy," *American Economic Review* 34, no. 1, part 2, Supplement, Papers and Proceedings of the Fifty-sixth Annual Meeting of the American Economic Association (March 1944): 305–14. Cited in Jon Hanf and Vera Belaya, "The 'Dark' and the 'Bright' Sides of Power in Supply Chain Networks," in 48th Annual Conference, Bonn, Germany, September 24–26, 2008, no. 52653. German Association of Agricultural Economists (GEWISOLA), http://ageconsearch.umn.edu/bitstream/52653/2/hanf.pdf.
11. Felix Berenskoetter, "Thinking about Power," in *Power in World Politics*, ed. Felix Berenskoetter and M. J. Williams (New York: Routledge, 2007), 10.
12. Robert O. Keohane and Joseph S. Nye, *Power and Interdependence* (Boston: Little, Brown, 1977).
13. Martha Finnemore, *National Interests in International Society* (Ithaca, NY: Cornell University Press, 1996).
14. Martha Finnemore and Kathryn Sikkink, "International Norm Dynamics and Political Change," *International Organization* 52, no. 4 (Autumn 1998): 887–917.
15. Richard Rosecrance, "The European Union: A New Type of International Actor," in *Paradoxes of European Foreign Policy*, ed. Jan Zielonka (The Hague: Kluwer Law International, 1998), 22.
16. Göran Therborn, "Europe in the Twenty-first Century," in *The Question of Europe*, ed. Peter Gowan and Perry Anderson (London: Verso, 1997), 380.
17. Manners, "Normative Power Europe," 235–258; and Ian Manners, "The European Union as a Normative Power: A Response to Thomas Diez," *Millennium* 35, no. 2 (2006): 167–180. In Tocci, *Who Is a Normative Foreign Policy Actor?*
18. See Martti Koskenniemi, *From Apology to Utopia: The Structure of International Legal Argument* (Cambridge: Cambridge University Press, 2005), 25–26.
19. Finnemore and Sikkink, "International Norm Dynamics and Political Change," 895–917.
20. Daniel S. Hamilton, "The United States: A Normative Power?" in Tocci, *Who Is a Normative Foreign Policy Actor?* 80.
21. Wolfers, "Goals of Foreign Policy."
22. Nancy Fraser, "Foucault on Modern Power: Empirical Insights and Normative Confusions," *PRAXIS International*, no. 3 (1981): 278.

23. Tocci, *Who Is a Normative Foreign Policy Actor?*
24. Christine Ingebritsen, "Norm Entrepreneurs Scandinavia's Role in World Politics," *Cooperation and Conflict: Journal of the Nordic International Studies Association* 37, no. 1 (2002): 11–23.
25. UN International Law Commission, Study Group on Fragmentation of International Law, Martti Koskenniemi, Chairman, "Fragmentation of International Law: Difficulties Arising from the Diversification and Expansion of International Law: Report of the Study Group of the International Law Commission / Finalized by Martti Koskenniemi, (A/CN.4/L.682)," April 13, 2006, http://www.un.org/en/ga/search/view_doc.asp?symbol=A/CN.4/L.682.
26. Robert Keohane and David G. Victor, "The Regime Complex for Climate Change," *Perspectives on Politics* 9, no. 1 (2011): 7–23; Joseph Nye Jr., "The Regime Complex for Managing Global Cyber Activities," Global Commission on International Governance, Paper Series, no. 1 (May 2014), https://www.cigionline.org/sites/default/files/gcig_paper_no1.pdf.
27. Joseph S. Nye Jr., *The Future of Power* (New York: Public Affairs, 2011), 114–18.
28. Xue Hanqin, *Chinese Contemporary Perspectives on International Law: History, Culture and International Law* (Leiden: Martinus Nijhoff Publishers, 2012).
29. On soft law and hard law, see, e.g., Oscar Schachter, "The Twilight Existence of Nonbinding International Agreements," *American Journal of International Law* 71, no. 2 (April 1977): 296, 299; Gunther F. Handl, W. Michael Reisman, Bruno Simma, Pierre Marie Dupuy, and Cristine Chinkin, "A Hard Look at Soft Law," *Proceedings of the Annual Meeting (American Society International Law)* 82 (April 20–23, 1988): 371, 376; John F. Murphy, *The Evolving Dimensions of International Law* (Cambridge: Cambridge University Press, 2010); and Fabien Terpan, "Soft Law in the European Union—The Changing Nature of EU Law," *European Law Journal* 21, no. 1 (2015): 68–96.
30. Terpan, "Soft Law in the European Union," 8–9. See also K. W. Abbott, R. O. Keohane, A. Moravcsik, A.-M. Slaughter, and D. Snidal, "The Concept of Legalization," *International Organization* 54, no. 3 (2002): 401–19.
31. In parallel, the UN also runs discussions on international norms and the developments in space technology (see A/RES/69/31 Prevention of Arms Race in Oputer Space) and use of unmanned vehicles and weapons (see A/RES/63/182 and A/69/642).
32. UN General Assembly, *Developments in the Field of Information and Telecommunications in the context of International Security: Resolution / Adopted by the General Assembly (A/RES/56/19)* (New York: UN, January 7, 2002), para. 4, http://www.un.org/en/ga/search/view_doc.asp?symbol=A/RES/56/19. The UN secretary-general appoints members of the UN GGE on the basis of equitable geographical distribution. The group meets in three to four weeklong sessions during the year and reports to the General Assembly on consensus basis.
33. UN Secretary-General and UN Group of Governmental Experts on Developments in the Field of Information and Telecommunications in the Context of International Security, *Group of Governmental Experts on Developments in the Field of Information and Telecommunications in the Context of International Security: note / by the Secretary-General (A/65/201)* (New York: UN, July 30, 2010), para. 18, http://www.un.org/en/ga/search/view_doc.asp?symbol=A/65/201.
34. Ibid.
35. UN Secretary-General and UN GGE, *GGE on Developments in the Field of Information and Telecommunications (A/70/174)*, paras. 9 and 10.
36. U.S. Department of Defense, "Department of Defense Strategy for Operating in Cyberspace," July 2011, http:/csrc.nist.gov/groups/SMA/ispab/documents/DOD-Strategy-for-Operating-in-Cyberspace.pdf.
37. Plainly, the utility of LOAC has been summarized as potentially motivating the enemy to

observe the same rules or surrender, guarding against acts that violate basic tenets of civilization, protecting against unnecessary suffering, and safeguarding certain fundamental human rights, providing advance notice of the accepted limits of warfare, reducing confusion, and making identification of violations more efficient. See Richard P. DiMeglio, Sean M. Condron, Owen B. Bishop, Gregory S. Musselman, Todd L. Lindquist, Andrew D. Gillman, William J. Johnson, and Daniel E. Stigall, *Law of Armed Conflict Deskbook* (Charlottesville, VA: International and Operational Law Department, U.S. Army Judge Advocate General's Legal Center and School, 2012), 9, https://www.loc.gov/rr/frd/Military_Law/pdf/LOAC-Deskbook-2012.pdf.

38. See U.S. State Department "Statement on the Consensus Achieved by the UN Group of Governmental Experts on Cyber Issues": "The United States is pleased to join consensus to affirm the applicability of international law to cyberspace. With that clear affirmation, this consensus sends a strong signal: States must act in cyberspace under the established international rules and principles that have guided their actions for decades—in peacetime and during conflict." Jen Psaki, "Statement on Consensus Achieved by the UN Group of Governmental Experts on Cyber Issues," June 7, 2013, http://www.state.gov/r/pa/prs/ps/2013/06/210418.htm.

39. Article 19: 1. Everyone shall have the right to hold opinions without interference. 2. Everyone shall have the right to freedom of expression; this right shall include freedom to seek, receive and impart information and ideas of all kinds, regardless of frontiers, either orally, in writing or in print, in the form of art, or through any other media of his choice.

40. 3. The exercise of the rights provided for in paragraph 2 of this article carries with it special duties and responsibilities. It may therefore be subject to certain restrictions, but these shall only be such as are provided by law and are necessary: (a) For respect of the rights or reputations of others; (b) For the protection of national security or of public order (order public), or of public health or morals.

41. Koskenniemi, *From Apology to Utopia*, 25.

42. "U.S. Reservations, Declarations, and Understandings, International Covenant on Civil and Political Rights, 138 Cong. Rec. S4781-01 (daily ed., April 2, 1992)," available at the University of Minnesota Human Rights Library website, http://www1.umn.edu/humanrts/usdocs/civilres.html.

43. U.S. Constitution Amendment I (1789, coming into force 1791): "Congress shall make no law respecting an establishment of religion, or prohibiting the free exercise thereof; or abridging the freedom of speech, or of the press; or the right of the people peaceably to assemble, and to petition the government for a redress of grievances." There are numerous state and federal statutes that seek to ensure the full extent of the guarantee of the First Amendment, such as the Freedom of Information Act and the Privacy Act.

44. ITU, "Signatories of the Final Acts: 89," http://www.itu.int/osg/wcit-12/highlights/signatories.html.

45. "U.S. Contributions to the World Conference on International Telecommunications (WCIT-12)," U.S. Department of State, August 3, 2012, http://www.state.gov/e/eb/rls/othr/telecom/196031.htm; and Michael Daniel, R. David Edelman, and Tom Power, "United behind the Free Flow of Information," White House blog, December 11, 2012, https://www.whitehouse.gov/blog/2012/12/11/united-behind-free-flow-information. See also Mike Masnick, "ITU Boss in Denial: Claims Success, Misrepresents Final Treaty, as US, UK, Canada and Many More Refuse to Sign," *techdirt*, December 14, 2012, https://www.techdirt.com/articles/20121214/05385721386/itu-boss-denial-claims-success-misrepresents-final-treaty-as-us-uk-canada-many-more-refuse-to-sign.shtml.

46. China, Kazakhstan, Kyrgyzstan, Russian Federation, Tajikistan, and Uzbekistan, *Letter Dated 9 January 2015 from the Permanent Representatives of China, Kazakhstan, Kyrgyzstan, Russian Federation, Tajikistan and*

Uzbekistan to the United Nations addressed to the Secretary-General (A/69/723) (other title, "International Code of Conduct for Information Security") (New York: UN, January 22, 2015), para. 7, http://www.un.org/en/ga/search/view_doc.asp?symbol=A/69/723; and Ministry of Foreign Affairs of the Russian Federation, "Information Security Doctrine of the Russian Federation," http://archive.mid.ru//bdomp/ns-osndoc.nsf/1e5f0de28fe77fdcc32575d900298676/2deaa9ee15ddd24bc32575d9002c442b!OpenDocument.

47. UN Secretary-General, Australia, Georgia, Germany, Greece, Kazakhstan, Netherlands, United States, *Developments in the Field of Information and Telecommunications in the Context of International Security: Report of the Secretary-General (A/66/152)* (New York: UN, July 15, 2011), 17, http://www.un.org/en/ga/search/view_doc.asp?symbol=A/66/152.
48. The United States, in particular, has taken the view that ILC draft articles do not represent customary law insofar as they contain "unsupported restrictions on the use of countermeasures." See U.S. Department of State, "Draft Articles on State Responsibility Comments of the Government of the United States of America," March 1, 2001, http://www.state.gov/documents/organization/28993.pdf.
49. UN Secretary-General and UN GGE, *GGE on Developments in the Field of Information and Telecommunications (A/70/174)*, para 28 (f).
50. "UN Cybersecurity Report Compromises on Self-Defense Issue," *Sputnik International*, August 17, 2015, http://sputniknews.com/politics/20150817/1025819426/UN-cybersecurity-report-compromises-on-self-defence.html. See also Colin S. Gray, *The Future of Strategy* (London: Polity, 2015), 4, on imprudence to demonize current state antagonists when there is little convincing evidence of serious misbehavior.
51. UN Secretary-General and UN GGE, *GGE on Developments in the Field of Information and Telecommunications (A/70/174)*, paras 13 (c) and (e).
52. "The development of norms for state conduct in cyberspace does not require a reinvention of customary international law, nor does it render existing international norms obsolete. Long-standing international norms guiding state behavior—in times of peace and conflict—also apply in cyberspace. Nonetheless, unique attributes of networked technology require additional work to clarify how these norms apply and what additional understandings might be necessary to supplement them. We will continue to work internationally to forge consensus regarding how norms of behavior apply to cyberspace, with the understanding that an important first step in such efforts is applying the broad expectations of peaceful and just interstate conduct to cyberspace." "International Strategy for Cyberspace: Prosperity, Security, and Openness in a Networked World," White House, May 2011, 9, https://www.whitehouse.gov/sites/default/files/rss_viewer/international_strategy_for_cyberspace.pdf.
53. Dimitar Kostadinov, "U.S. Cyber Policy—Course and Legal Aspects," INFOSEC Institute, undated, http://resources.infosecinstitute.com/u-s-cyber-policy-course-and-legal-aspects/.
54. "Executive Order—Promoting International Regulatory Cooperation," White House, May 1, 2012, https://www.whitehouse.gov/the-press-office/2012/05/01/executive-order-promoting-international-regulatory-cooperation.
55. Andrey S. Makarychev, "Rebranding Russia: Norms, Politics and Power," in Tocci, *Who Is a Normative Foreign Policy Actor?* 161, 202.
56. Ibid., 203.
57. Andrey Krutskikh and Anatoly Streltsov, "International Law and the Problem of International Information Security," *International Affairs* 60, no. 6 (2014): 65.
58. Government of Kenya, Ministry of Information Communications and Technology, "Cybersecurity Strategy," Government of Kenya, 2014, http://www.itu.int/en/ITU-D/Cybersecurity/Documents/National_Strategies_Repository/Kenya_2014_GOK-national-cybersecurity-strategy.pdf.
59. "Key note: Marina Kaljurand, Undersecretary for Political Affairs, Ministry of For-

eign Affairs of Estonia," EuroDIG, December 17, 2015, http://eurodigwiki.org/wiki/Key_note:_Marina_Kaljurand,_Undersecretary_for_Political_Affairs,_Ministry_of_Foreign_Affairs_of_Estonia.

60. "Global Conference on Cyberspace 2015: Chair's Statement," paras. 33–34, https://www.gccs2015.com/sites/default/files/documents/Chairs%20Statement%20GCCS2015%20-%2017%20April.pdf.

61. "ICRC-AALCO Special Issue on Cyber Warfare & IHL Launched in Beijing," International Committee of the Red Cross, April 23, 2015, http://blogs.icrc.org/new-delhi/2015/04/23/journal-cyber-warfare-international-humanitarian-law/. The conference was arranged in Beijing parallel to The Hague GCCS conference.

Country in Focus

Inter-Korean Rivalry in the Cyber Domain

The North Korean Cyber Threat in the *Sŏn'gun* Era

Daniel A. Pinkston

The Democratic People's Republic of Korea (DPRK or North Korea) is an authoritarian state now ruled by the third generation of the Kim family dynasty. Since its establishment in September 1948, the DPRK has been locked in an intense rivalry with the Republic of Korea (ROK or South Korea). The Korean War (1950–1953) ended in an armistice, but on several occasions, there have been fears that crises would plunge the peninsula back into wartime conditions. Since the end of the Korean War, the technological and military capabilities of the two Koreas have changed considerably. Cyber weapons and cyber tools for conducting network operations in cyberspace are relatively new, and many analysts and policymakers are grappling with the way these instruments affect or potentially affect statecraft and conflict. North Korea's cyber capabilities and growing potential to wage asymmetric warfare warrant a continuous assessment of DPRK motivations, ideology, doctrine, objectives, and military capabilities, including in the cyber domain.

According to its current constitution, the DPRK is a socialist state based on the ideology and leadership exploits of Kim Il-sung and Kim Jong-il. Its territory includes the whole Korean peninsula and its surrounding islands, and its government represents the interests of all the Korean people. Under this formulation, the ROK is illegitimate and inter-Korean relations are a zero-sum rivalry. All DPRK state activities must be done under the guidance of the Korean Workers Party.[1]

Generally, North Korea's political, social, and economic systems closely resemble classical communist systems of the twentieth century, including a single political party, democratic-centralism, and an intrusive state that controls economic transactions and social relationships.[2] However, North Korea fought a fratricidal war with the South and has survived despite the collapse of socialism in the former Eastern bloc and a horrific famine in the mid-1990s. The DPRK has thus modified its state ideology into a more militant version of traditional Marxism-Leninism[3] to explain and account for the collapse of socialism elsewhere and to shore up the revolutionary zeal of North Koreans who must "complete the revolution by liberating the South."[4] Under leader Kim Jong-un, "*sŏn'gun* revolutionary ideology will create a new path to advance great socialist achievements and the road to victory."[5]

In June 1950 North Korea tried to unify the country by force but failed despite sig-

---

Daniel A. Pinkston is a lecturer in international relations at Troy University. Previously, he was the Northeast Asia deputy project director for the International Crisis Group in Seoul and the director of the East Asia Nonproliferation Program at the James Martin Center for Nonproliferation Studies.

nificant military and geopolitical advantages at that time. The North recovered more quickly from the war, but by the late 1970s the North Korean economy began to exhibit the typical inefficiencies of central planning,[6] and Pyongyang began to fall behind Seoul in economic performance. The North's economic decline accelerated with the termination of Soviet subsidies in the early 1990s, leading to a decline in the state's formal economic sector.[7] Since then, the inter-Korean balance of power has shifted drastically against Pyongyang. South Korea's population of 50 million is twice that of the North, while its economic output is now about forty-five times its northern neighbor.[8] South Korea also enjoys the support of the United States, its ally since the Korean War.

This shift has pushed North Korea to rely increasingly on asymmetric capabilities to support its strategic objectives. North Korea allocates a tremendous amount of resources to its military and maintains about 300 weapons and munitions factories,[9] in addition to stockpiles the South Korea Defense Ministry estimates would be depleted in only one to three months of war.[10] With its ability to secure military objectives rapidly hindered by inferior conventional weapon systems, Pyongyang has shifted its focus to devote more resources on the development of asymmetric capabilities, including biological, chemical, and nuclear weapons, as well as ballistic missiles, submarines, long-range artillery, special operations forces, underground tunnels, electronic warfare, and cyber warfare.[11] North Korean military planners and strategists are mindful of the unfavorable conventional balance, so the [North] Korean People's Army (KPA) frequently conducts joint training to prepare for the integration of ground, naval, and air forces with its asymmetric capabilities to compensate for conventional weaknesses.[12]

North Korean military doctrine prescribes a quick offensive in order to achieve military objectives before U.S. reinforcements can support South Korea. North Korea has conducted cyber attacks and cyber espionage against South Korea in the past, but in the case of an inter-Korean military conflict, cyber warfare almost certainly would be integrated with electronic warfare measures, such as Global Positioning System (GPS) jamming,[13] to degrade South Korean and U.S. systems for navigation and intelligence, surveillance, and reconnaissance. During the November 2010 artillery attack against Yŏnp'yŏng Island, for example, the KPA reportedly jammed South Korea's artillery acquisition radars, disrupting the South's counterfire.[14]

North Korea's cyber and electronic capabilities could also provide it with an opportunity to create confusion in the South before mobilizing KPA forces and reserve units, enhancing the element of surprise and working to the North's advantage. However, North Korea is not merely integrating its cyber capabilities with other weapon systems to fight a war. It has also pursued cyber espionage, psychological operations (influence operations), and cyber crime.[15] To better understand North Korean cyber activities, it is necessary to clearly assess the country's motivations and the way its cyber capabilities mesh with other capabilities Pyongyang utilizes to pursue state goals.[16] Furthermore, these motivations and comprehensive attributes of national power should be placed in the context of the political, economic, military, industrial, technological, and social dimensions that affect North Korea's capabilities and activities in the cyber domain.[17]

Given extensive state control and the absence of a civil society, all North Korean cyber activities are conducted under state guidance. North Korea's extremely authoritarian political system is characterized by the inability of all political actors to make credible commitments. Political differences are resolved through violence or the threat of violence. The only way to oust the dictator is through force, and since everyone—including the dictator—knows this, the dictator must be prepared to use any means necessary to deter or crush rebellions.[18] The dictator must control the state security apparatus, institutions specializing in violence and repression. Institutional design matters in authoritarian systems because a concentration of power in a single internal security institution could lead to it turning on the dictator.[19] To reduce the likelihood of a coup d'état, the North Korean security apparatus is well developed, with internal redundancies and agencies that compete for patronage while monitoring each other and blocking rivals from executing an insurrection. In the information technology (IT) realm, there are technical reasons for a division of labor among different institutions. But in the North Korean case, if the means to control information were concentrated in a single institution, that privilege would be very valuable if it were to turn against the regime.

North Korea's IT Background and Capabilities

North Korea's economic deprivation and backwardness have been well documented, but the state has sustained development in a small number of sectors, including IT and telecommunications. Pyongyang first demonstrated a serious interest in an indigenous IT sector in 1979, when it sought the establishment of an integrated circuit plant through a project sponsored by the United Nations Development Program (UNDP) and the UN Industrial Development Organization.[20]

The foundation for North Korea's cyber warfare capabilities was laid in the 1980s. In 1983 North Korea established its first computer assembly plant, and two years later, it opened an electronic computation college.[21] In 1986 the Pyongyang Informatics Center (PIC) was established to create automated systems and software for industrial processes.[22] That same year, North Korea reportedly hired twenty-five Soviet instructors to train "cyber-warriors" at the Mirim Command Automation College (later changed to the Kim Il Military College).[23] In 1990 the Korea Computer Center (KCC) was established, and subsequently it has expanded in capacity.[24]

North Korea's interest in cyber warfare increased with technological advances and the collapse of the Soviet Union. During the 1990s, the KPA studied the "electronic intelligence warfare" concepts formulated by China's People's Liberation Army, which had observed the role of electronic warfare and cyber operations during the first Persian Gulf War and North Atlantic Treaty Organization (NATO) operations in the Balkans.[25] The year 1995 marked a turning point for the KPA and cyber warfare when leader Kim Jong-il issued his often-cited directive for the KPA General Staff to develop cyber warfare capabilities. Kim reportedly said, "In the 20th century, war is with bullets over oil. But in the 21st century, war will be [fought as] information warfare."[26]

In 1996 the first known Internet link between North Korea and the outside world was established through the Pyongyang office of the UNDP. The same year, work began on *kwangmyŏng*, North Korea's national intranet, linking government agencies, academic institutions, and research institutes. At the same time, fiber-optic cables were installed to connect military installations.[27] In 1998 Kim issued another directive to the KPA General Staff to pursue cyber warfare capabilities.[28]

The KPA does not publish official doctrines, so beliefs about North Korean cyber doctrine must be inferred from media, academic journals, defector testimony, and analysis of past behavior and cyber incidents.[29] According to scholar Alexandre Mansourov, KPA theoreticians view cyber warfare (싸이버戰) and cyber war (싸이버戰爭) as different concepts. "Cyber warfare," Mansourov writes, "is one of the methods of the conduct of war," whereas "cyber war is a way to affect the enemy's will and force him to do what one wants."[30] Similarly, the KPA views cyber warfare as distinct from electronic warfare (EW) and signals intelligence (SIGINT) and as comprising "elements of electronic intelligence warfare, computer network warfare (NW), psychological warfare (influence operations), and military deception and information warfare (IW)."[31]

Despite a lack of official documentation, Pyongyang has obviously invested in cyber capabilities and established cyber institutions to support state objectives. In sum, cyber capabilities are attractive to North Korea given its relative conventional military weakness, the low development costs of cyber capabilities, attribution difficulties, and the almost certain benefits in the realm of espionage. When discerning or assessing North Korean activities or behavior in cyberspace, the KWP policy lines and objectives are a good place to start.[32]

Tools, Techniques, and Processes

There are several types of cyber tools or cyber weapons, which scholars and analysts classify in slightly different ways.[33] Furthermore, cyber attacks often are difficult to trace since skilled operators can obscure the origin by launching attacks remotely from other computers in cyberspace. This makes it difficult to assess North Korea's cyber capabilities because the origins of cyber incidents are often difficult to determine with high confidence. This attribution problem can also provide governments with plausible deniability when they blame "patriotic hackers" or "hactivists" for cyber incidents.[34] In the North Korean case, however, the state tightly limits Internet access,[35] so cyber activity originating from North Korean territory is almost certainly conducted by the state or with state support.[36]

The U.S. military classifies cyber activities under a Computer Network Operations (CNO) rubric.[37] Under this general template, North Korea's CNO fall into the following categories:

- Computer network attack (CNA)
- Computer network exploitation (CNE)
- Computer network defense (CND)
- Influence operations
  - Military information support operations (MISO)
  - Information operations (IO)
  - Propaganda
- Cyber crime
- Cyber terrorism
- Cyber (physical) weapons

The following sections examine each branch of North Korea's CNO with reference to its possible utility during an inter-Korean conflict.

Computer Network Attack

CNA is designed to disrupt, degrade, or prevent the enemy from operating in cyberspace and can include the destruction of data within enemy computer networks. Military networks are a primary target,[38] but critical infrastructure, such as financial and banking networks, utilities, and communication systems, also could be targeted during an inter-Korean conflict. The private sector owns much of the telecommunications hardware and networks that form the superstructure of the cyber domain, but these systems are used by governments, militaries, private firms, and civil society. Much of the critical infrastructure—such as hospitals, banks, transportation systems, and the power grid—are privately owned but nevertheless critical to national security. The dual-use nature of cyberspace often makes it difficult to determine who should be responsible for cybersecurity. Private firms often underestimate cyber risks and under invest in cybersecurity or prefer to "free-ride" while expecting the government to manage the North Korean cyber threat.

Computer Network Exploitation

North Korea has been very active in the realm of CNE, the process of gathering data from enemy information systems or networks.[39] Pyongyang has an advantage in using cyber means to collect open source intelligence (OSINT) on the South. South Korea's high rate of connectivity and open society provide excellent opportunities for data collection, including potential targets for phishing, spear phishing, and whaling attacks. Logical (cyber) weapons can be combined with physical security lapses to target specific networks or data. Many of these logical weapons are available for free on the Internet, but more sophisticated varieties are developed by state-sponsored programs. These logical weapons include reconnaissance, scanning, access, and escalation tools, and exfiltration, sustainment, assault, and obfuscation tools.[40]

In February 2016 a consortium of cybersecurity firms led by Novetta Solutions, a Virginia-based advanced analytics company that frequently contracts for the U.S. government, published a report called "Operation Blockbuster." The report analyzed the cyber attack against Sony Pictures Entertainment that took place in November 2014, an attack the Federal Bureau of Investigations (FBI) blamed on North Korea.[41] It attributed the attack to the "Lazarus Group," a mysterious cyber-crime collective to which numerous recent cyber attacks have been linked. Although Operation Blockbuster declined to name North Korea as responsible for the attack, the results were not inconsistent with the FBI's conclusions. After several months scanning and analyzing billions of computer code files, the Novetta consortium determined that the malware tools used in the Sony attack match those used in other attacks over the past seven years at least.[42] The report concluded that the Lazarus Group, which almost certainly must be North Korea, has

> a wide spectrum of CNO capabilities, including distributed denial of service (DDoS) malware, keyloggers, remote access Trojans (RATs), and even a peer-to-peer (P2P) malware that allows operators to establish a common program base and remote administration across all infected machines.[43]

Computer Network Defense

Little is known about North Korea's capabilities in the realm of CND, which according to the U.S. Department of Defense (DoD), "aims to protect, monitor, analyze, detect[,] and respond to unauthorized activity within . . . information systems and computer networks."[44] But the country's low online connectivity—the lowest in the world—makes it less vulnerable in cyberspace than its southern neighbor.[45] Many South Korean officials and analysts lament that the North's relative invulnerability obviates the possibility of deterring North Korean cyber attacks through threat of retaliation in kind. However, North Korea is not completely cut off from the global Internet. And as the case of the Stuxnet attack against Iran's uranium enrichment facilities demonstrated, even "air-gapped" networks can be penetrated by human compromising of physical security protocols.

During a visit to Pyongyang in 2012, I observed a wall poster inside the Grand People's Study House informing visitors of an "IPS" (intrusion prevention system) that was a "new network security method to monitor and remove all attack and intrusion viruses in materials and files sent over the network." These types of measures and alerts would not be necessary if no viruses or worms existed in the North. However, computer users in North Korea are probably quite vulnerable to malware because they use unlicensed or out-of-date software and because of the likely widespread sharing of portable storage devices such as memory sticks.

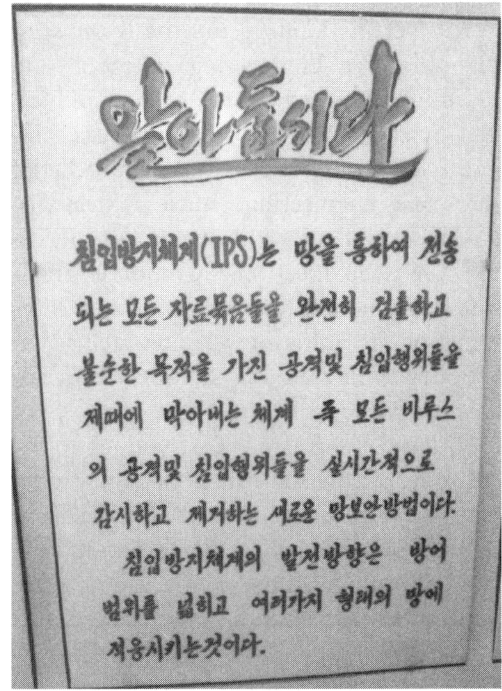

Poster in Grand People's Study House, June 2012. *Photo by Daniel A. Pinkston.*

Influence Operations

Ideology and propaganda play a prominent role in North Korean domestic politics, and the regime emphasizes the importance of influence operations in promoting its political and social system to South Koreans. Furthermore, Pyongyang believes that "it is in a struggle with international imperialism over political ideology" and that it must use the Internet to promote the "genuine qualities of [North Korean] socialism" internationally.[46]

North and South Korea have been engaged in a soft-power battle for influence since the peninsula was divided at the end of World War II. The inter-Korean struggle for influence has not been limited to the Korean peninsula, but has played out in the region and internationally as well.[47] North Korean propaganda and psychological operations have naturally moved into cyberspace. Before the Internet era, the South simply jammed the frequencies of North Korean radio and television broadcasts, and the National Security Act has broadly prohibited the possession of "anti-state" reading materials in the South.[48] But cyberspace is much more porous, which has posed policy dilemmas for Seoul's management of Pyongyang's influence operations. Some South Koreans advocate draconian measures to block North Korean content in cyberspace, especially during an inter-Korean crisis or war.[49]

North Korea has established about 160 websites that are hosted abroad and recently has begun hosting a few websites in the DPRK itself, such as the homepage for the Korean Central News Agency (KCNA). North Korea has a news channel on YouTube.com, and the KWP's Committee for the Peaceful Reunification of the Fatherland has a website and an official Twitter account, as well as a multitude of North Korean accounts posing as South Koreans or as members of the Korean diaspora. North Korea reportedly tasks over 300 people with writing comments for websites and on social media to promote the North and discredit the South.[50] Notably, North Korea increased its influence operations in cyberspace following the March 2010 sinking of the ROKS *Ch'ŏnan*, a South Korean warship, in the Yellow Sea and the subsequent release of a South Korean–sponsored international report that found Pyongyang responsible.[51]

Cyber (Physical) Weapons

Cyber weapons are malware that cause physical damage by altering the commands in software operating machinery, pipelines, industrial equipment, dams, weapons, and other infrastructure. The result is similar to that caused by a kinetic device. The most notable examples include the explosion of a Soviet pipeline in 1982 caused by the reported insertion of Trojan malware by the United States, the reported malfunction of Syrian air defense radar during the Israeli air raid against a Syrian nuclear reactor construction site in 2007, and the Stuxnet worm reportedly created by the United States and Israel to damage Iranian uranium-enrichment centrifuges between 2009 and 2010.[52]

Malware can be inserted into programmable logic controllers (PLC)—computers designed for the automation of machinery—or supervisory control and data acquisition systems (SCADA) used for remote monitoring and control of the power grid or water and gas flows in pipelines. Theoretically, malware can take control of these systems and cause physical damage, but this is not easy to achieve. There is no evidence that North Korea has developed or deployed this type of malware, but there is probably no way to know until it activates.

North Korean Cyber Institutions

The most important aspect of any country's cyber-warfare and cybersecurity capabilities is its human resources. North Korea has been identifying young students for specialization in computers since the 1990s. Middle school students nationwide are selected for special regional schools, and the top students are sent to Pyongyang No. 1 Middle School and the Kŭmsŏng No. 1 and No. 2 Middle Schools for training in computer science. The brightest are then able to enter top universities such as Kim Il-sung University, Kim Chaek University of Technology, Pyongyang Computer Technology University, Kim Il-sung Military Academy, and the Kim Il Military Academy.[53]

In June 1964 North Korea established the Second Academy of Natural Sciences, which is responsible for the research and development of weapon systems. The academy has over fifty research institutes and about 15,000 researchers. The Pyongyang National Defense College and the Ryongsŏng Light Electrical Engineering College also are subordinate to the Second Academy of Natural Sciences. The academy, colleges, and research institutes mostly focus on rocketry, aerospace engineering, nuclear weapons, guidance systems, and materials science. However, the Electronic Computer Institute also conducts research on computer automation programs for weapon systems.[54] In October 1985 Kim Jong-il visited the academy with then-chief of the General Staff O Gŭng-yŏl and issued instructions to increase research on missiles, electronic warfare, and long-range artillery.[55] The academy provides direct support for electronic warfare and indirect support for cyber warfare through research and training in the realms of electronics and electrical engineering.

Kim Il-sung University is North Korea's most prestigious academic institution with the country's brightest students.[56] The university's seven colleges include one dedicated to computer science, which trains students in software development, network management, and network security. The Faculty of Electronics and Automation became independent of the College of Computer Science in 2010.[57] The faculty educates students in the fields of automation, which includes PLC and SCADA systems for industry. The university's Information Technology Institute is dedicated to the development of IT and software, including antivirus programs.[58]

The Kim Il Military Academy, established in 1986, is another important educational institute for the training of North Korean cyber warriors. The college has a five-year program to train students in programming, command automation, computation, technical reconnaissance, and electronic warfare. The college develops programs for computer network defense in addition to malware for computer network attacks and produces about 120 graduates every year, most of them assigned to the Reconnaissance General Bureau (RGB), electronic warfare units under the General Staff, military colleges, the Guard Command, or units tasked with "liaison missions" and influence operations toward the South.[59]

The Korea Computer Center (KCC), established in 1990, has developed software and operating systems. In 1996 the KCC was elevated to the status of a cabinet ministry, and it now serves as the content-screening authority for North Korea's national intranet. The KCC has been suspected of involvement in computer network operations in the past, but most of its activities appear to be in the commercial and nonmilitary realms. According to South Korea's Science and Technology Policy Institute, the KCC was under the "IT Command" until March or April 2015 when it was placed under the National Defense Commission's Department 91, which also took control of the Pyongyang Informatics Center, the Pyongyang Kwangmyŏng IT Service Center, the Noŭn Technology Joint Venture Company, and the Advanced Technology Service Center. The change apparently was made to ensure tighter state control of information and communications technology (ICT).[60] However, in June 2016 the DPRK revised its constitution to establish the State Affairs Commission (SAC), which has replaced the National Defense Commission (NDC). According to the South Korean Ministry of Unification, the KCC has a total staff of about 2,000.[61]

Computer network operations are split between the KPA General Staff and the RGB. Nominally, the General Staff is subordinate to the Ministry of the People's Armed Forces, but during wartime it comes under direct control of the KPA supreme commander. The RGB, which also had been directly subordinate to the NDC prior to the 2016 constitutional revision, is responsible for missions including intelligence and CNO against the South.[62]

The General Staff's Electronic Warfare Department, also known as the Command Automation Department, is responsible for military communications and electronic warfare operations. The department has two brigade-level electronic warfare units with about 600 staff members each, one in Sangwŏn, South P'yŏng'an Province and one in Nampo City. The department maintains Command Automation Sections at each army corps in the forward area near the Demilitarized Zone. These corps-based units are staffed with about 60–100 personnel and are likely responsible for the previously mentioned GPS jamming operations.[63]

The Command Automation Department also develops software with its Office 31 developing hacking tools, Office 32 developing military-related software, and Office 56 developing software for command and control communications. Each of these offices is staffed with about 50–60 KPA officers.[64] The General Staff also manages the Enemy Operations Department, which has Office 204 under its command. Office 204 conducts influence operations using phishing e-mails against the South Korean military.[65]

The RGB, also known as KPA Unit 586, was directly subordinate to the NDC prior its replacement by the SAC.[66] The RGB conducts intelligence and special operations against the South and is believed to be responsible for the torpedo attack that sank the ROKS *Ch'ŏnan*. The United States sanctioned the RGB in January 2015 following the 2014 Sony cyber attack.[67]

The RGB's Department 121, also known as the Electronic Reconnaissance Department or the Cyber Warfare Guidance Department, conducts computer network attacks and exfiltration operations and is staffed with about 3,000 personnel. The RGB also controls a cyber attack unit known as Office 91, in addition to Office 31 and Office 32, which conduct influence operations against South Korean citizens through e-mail phishing. The Data Investigation Examination Office conducts cyber espionage to collect intelligence on politics, economics, and societies abroad.[68]

The RGB's 110 Institute, also known as the Technical Reconnaissance Group, conducts computer network operations against military units and strategic organizations. The 110 Institute has sent cyber operatives abroad to China in Shenyang, Dalian, Guangzhou, and Beijing in the guise of trading company employees to conduct cyber operations. The 110 Institute probably executed the attack against Sony as well as DDoS and malware attacks against South Korea in July 2009, March 2011, March and June 2013, and late 2014.[69]

The KWP's Unification and United Front Department is also active in cyber influence operations through social media and websites such as Uriminzokkiri, which is maintained by the party's Committee for the Peaceful Reunification of the Fatherland. Other entities—such as the Ministry of State Security and the Ministry of People's Security—likely have some cyber capabilities for internal monitoring, surveillance, and other operations.

Past Cyber Incidents Attributed to North Korea

It is uncertain when North Korea first began computer network operations against the South. But according to Kim Hŭng-gwang, executive director of NK Intellectuals Solidarity and a former computer science professor in North Korea, the first attack occurred in 2004.[70] The attribution problem also makes it difficult to prove North Korean culpability for these past attacks. However, cyber incidents in South Korea stretching back more than a decade are consistent with North Korean objectives, doctrine, and tactics. Furthermore, ongoing and persistent cyber conflicts do not emerge randomly; rather, cyber conflicts track entrenched international disputes.[71] The growing number of cyber incidents in South Korea, along with the expanding repository of cyber forensics, implies near-certain North Korean culpability.

North Korean cyber attacks have not abated, and we should expect them to continue in the shadow of what some scholars have called the "stability-instability paradox in cyberspace."[72] In other words, the costs of high-intensity conflict are so great that all actors have disincentives to escalate and are therefore deterred from taking actions that risk escalation. The paradox is that North Korea is not deterred from actions on the lower-end of the conflict spectrum such as cyber attacks. However, since the cyber domain is not bounded geographically in the same way that the land, sea, airspace, and outer space domains are, the Sony hacking incident demonstrates that North Korea can "export instability through cyber space."[73]

If past is prelude when it comes to North Korean cyber behavior, we should expect ongoing computer network operations across the full range of activities. The following are some of the most noteworthy cyber incidents attributed to North Korea:

- Operation Troy, 2009–2012[74]
- South Korean military secrets stolen
- DDoS attacks, July 2009[75]
- 270,000 zombie-computer botnet used in DDoS attack against thirty-five U.S. and South Korean websites including the Blue House and the White House
- "Ten Days of Rain," March 2011[76]
- 100,000 zombie-computer botnet used in DDoS attack against South Korean government, financial entities, and corporations and the U.S. military
- Nonghyŏp Bank attack, April 2011[77]
- Malware shutdown bank network and ATM service
- Dark Seoul attacks, March 2013[78]
- KBS, MBC, YTN, Shinhan Bank, Cheju Bank, Nonghyŏp Bank
- Sony Pictures, November 2014[79]
- Korea Hydro and Nuclear Power, December 2014[80]

Although North Korea may not be responsible for every cyber incident in the South, the responses and remedies are often the same regardless of the responsible party.[81]

Policy Implications: Remediation and Countermeasures

The policy implications in the cybersecurity realm are complicated by several factors. First, cyber operations cover a wide range of activities: espionage, crime, influence operations, terrorism, and physical weapons. Second, both the initiator and the target of cyber operations can be state or non-state actors with a multitude of motivations. Third, international and domestic laws are ambiguous or inadequate for dealing with many cybersecurity issues, leading to different interpretations of the legal framework. Fourth, the attribution problem, characterized by time-consuming and imperfect cyber forensics, hinders a timely and appropriate reaction. Fifth, computer networks—government, military, and private—are connected by an infrastructure that is owned by both states and private firms. In most countries, private firms own most critical infrastructure, such as power grids, dams, financial networks, communication systems, and hospitals, but governments consider critical infrastructure an essential element of national security.[82] The owners of critical infrastructure might underestimate cyber threats and underinvest in cybersecurity with the expectation that the government will provide the public good of cybersecurity. Sixth, cyber operations can circumvent international borders, create global problems, and require multilateral cooperation.

As South Korea becomes more dependent on Internet services, the North and other malicious actors can exploit the South's increasing vulnerabilities.[83] As scholars and policymakers struggle to design appropriate policy measures, their personal views and theoretical perspectives of cyber conflict influence their understanding.[84] Furthermore, policymakers grapple with the need to define cyber operations and place them in either the criminal justice system or the national security realm.[85] However, recurring cyber incidents, growing vulnerabilities, and the long shadow of the acute security dilemma in Korea are leading to greater securitization of Korean cyberspace.[86]

After suffering a series of cyber incidents,

South Korea is now establishing the institutional framework and human resources to address the North Korean cyber threat. In 2011 it established its "National Cyber Security Masterplan," which created an interagency and public-private partnership for countering cyber threats.[87] The Ministry of Science, ICT and Future Planning (MSIP) oversees interagency cybersecurity coordination through the Cyber Security Policy Bureau in the Office of ICT Policy. The MSIP also leads an ambitious national industrial policy effort in the ICT sector,[88] and the South Korean government likely understates the cybersecurity role of the National Intelligence Service (NIS) in the open source literature. In the case of North Korean cyber operations against the South, interagency cooperation includes the NIS, the Ministry of National Defense (MND), the Korea Internet and Security Agency (KISA), the Ministry of Unification, the Ministry of Public Safety and Security, the Blue House, and the Korean National Police. The MSIP has been coordinating with the MND and KISA to issue a five-level advisory on the national cybersecurity threat.[89]

Managing cybersecurity threats requires international cooperation, and South Korea's KISA is a steering committee member of the Asia Pacific Computer Emergency Response Team (APCERT).[90] KISA is best suited for alerting other members about North Korean malware and cyber operations given South Korea's experience and Korean language ability. One of APCERT's three supporting members, Microsoft, opened a cybersecurity center in Seoul in March 2016 to address cybersecurity threats with both the private sector and the government.[91]

If North Korea were to conduct cyber operations in coordination with a traditional kinetic military attack against the South or a cyber attack that caused physical damage and deaths, it would present grave challenges to Seoul and the international community. In the former case, military reprisals would be warranted under the UN Charter, and the United States would be obliged to fulfill its commitment to assist the South under the bilateral mutual defense treaty. However, in the latter case, there is a lack of clarity and consensus on the definition of the use of force or an armed attack in cyberspace. Some cyber operations, such as the crashing of civilian airliners and trains or the damaging of chemical plants and nuclear reactors resulting in casualties, would be considered armed attacks. However, most cyber operations, both in theory and in practice, do not meet this threshold.

These gray areas, as well as the nearly instantaneous speed of cyber operations, will pose extraordinary challenges for policymakers, military strategists, and cybersecurity specialists. Targets of cyber attacks have an incentive to execute robust counterstrikes through asymmetric or conventional means before suffering a catastrophic attack. However, targets of North Korean cyber operations have an incentive to exercise some restraint to prevent further harm to civilian targets throughout cyberspace.[92] Since cyber attacks raise serious concerns about escalation, South Korea and the United States will have to consider the laws of war, or *jus ad bellum* and *jus in bello*.[93] Furthermore, combatants are bound by international humanitarian law that requires states to exercise restraint according to the principles of distinction, proportionality, and precaution to minimize the risk to noncombatants in a theater of conflict.[94] In cases where North Korean cyber operations do not rise to the level of armed attacks, several delicate legal issues will complicate countermeasures that must align with the standards and principles of international law.[95]

As North Korea's conventional forces decline, cyber operations are ideal asymmetric strategies. To combat these capabilities, governments must maintain situational awareness to ascertain the severity of a cyber incident and qualify it as a force multiplier in coordination with a broader military attack or a prelude to subsequent cyber attacks. If critical infrastructure is paralyzed or degraded, governments and firms will need resilient backup systems to restore services. Moreover, the militaries of South Korea, the United States, and other United Nations Command sending states that participate in annual military exercises in Korea need to include North Korean cyber operations and responses thereto as regular parts of their training.[96] Preparation for the worst-case scenarios requires cooperation between governments and the private sector, along with interagency exercises and international cooperation.

Notes

1. 조선민주주의인민공화국 사회주의헌법 (2012) [Democratic People's Republic of Korea Socialist Constitution (2012)].
2. János Kornai, "Power," ch. 3 in *The Socialist System: The Political Economy of Communism* (Princeton, NJ: Princeton University Press, 1992).
3. János Kornai, "Ideology," ch. 4 in Ibid.
4. "조선로동당규약 서문 [Korean Workers Party Preamble]," revised at the 4th Party Conference, April 11, 2012.
5. 고 영 학, "선군혁명사상은 사회주의위업의 승리를 확고히 담보하는 위대한 사상," 김일성종합대학학보 (철학, 경제), 주체103 (2014)년 제60권 제9호.
6. János Kornai, *The Socialist System: The Political Economy of Communism* (Princeton, NJ: Princeton University Press, 1992).
7. Kim Suk-Jin and Yang Moon-Soo, "The Growth of the Informal Economy in North Korea," Study Series 15-02, KINU, October 2015.
8. Central Intelligence Agency, "World Fact Book," https://www.cia.gov/library/publications/resources/the-world-factbook/.
9. Republic of Korea Ministry of National Defense, *2014 Defense White Paper*, December 2014, 33.
10. Ibid.
11. Ibid., 27; and Duk-Ki Kim, "The Republic of Korea's Counter-Asymmetric Strategy," *Naval War College Review* 65, no. 1 (Winter 2012): 55–74.
12. 윤규식, "북한의 사이버전 능력과 위협 전망," 군사논단, 제68호, 2011 년 겨울, 74쪽.
13. The North has jammed GPS signals on at least four occasions since 2010, most recently in April 2016. "North Korea 'Jamming GPS Signals' Near South Border," BBC, April 1, 2016, http://www.bbc.com/news/world-asia-35940542; Choe Sang-hun, "North Korea Tried to Jam GPS Signals across Border, South Korea Says," *New York Times*, April 1, 2016, http://www.nytimes.com/2016/04/02/world/asia/north-korea-jams-gps-signals.html; "N. Korea Halts GPS Jamming: Gov't," *Korea Herald*, April 6, 2016, http://www.koreaherald.com/view.php?ud=20160406000972; and "S. Korea to Bolster GPS Signal Protection Amid N. Korean Threats," Yonhap News Agency, April 8, 2016, http://english.yonhapnews.co.kr/national/2016/04/08/28/0301000000AEN20160408005600320F.html.
14. 신석호 및 유성운, "[北, 연평도 포격 도발]軍, 전자전에 속수무책," 동아일보, 2010년 12월 3일, http://news.donga.com/BestClick/3/all/20101203/33035628/1.
15. 임종인, 권유중, 장규현, 백승조, "북한의 사이버전력 현황과 한국의 국가적 대응전략," 국방정책연구, 제29권, 제4호, 2013 겨울, 16-18쪽.
16. Jenny Jun, Scott LaFoy, and Ethan Sohn, "North Korea's Cyber Operations: Strategy and Responses," Center for Strategic and International Studies, December 2015; and HP Security Research, "Profiling an Enigma: The Mystery of North Korea's Cyber Threat Landscape," HP Security Briefing Episode 16, August 2014.
17. 김인수 및 KMARMA (김건일, 박상구,

박은석, 박주호, 이상언, 림피팁), "북한 사이버전 수행능력의 평가와 전망," 통일정책연구, 제24권 1호, 2015, 119쪽.

18. Georgy Epogorov and Konstantin Sonin, "Dictators and Their Viziers: Agency Problems in Dictatorships," William Davidson Institute Working Paper no. 735, January 2005; Paul Gregory, *Terror by Quota: State Security from Lenin to Stalin* (New Haven, CT: Yale University Press, 2009); Milan W. Svolik, *The Politics of Authoritarian Rule* (Cambridge: Cambridge University Press, 2012); and Ronald Wintrobe, *The Political Economy of Dictatorship* (Cambridge: Cambridge University Press, 1998).
19. See Gregory, *Terror by Quota*; and Paul R. Gregory, *The Political Economy of Stalinism: Evidence from the Soviet Secret Archives* (Cambridge: Cambridge University Press, 2003).
20. Peter Hayes, "DPRK Information Strategy—Does It Exist?" in *Bytes and Bullets: Information Technology Revolution and National Security on the Korean Peninsula*, ed. Alexandre Y. Mansourov (Honolulu: Asia-Pacific Center for Strategic Studies, 2005).
21. Ibid.
22. Ibid.
23. 윤규식, "북한의 사이버전 능력과 위협 전망," 군사논단, 제68호, 2011 년 겨울.
24. "[北 조선컴퓨터센터 성급기관 격상]," 조선일보, 2001년 2월 21일, http://nk.chosun.com/news/articleView.html?idxno=4301; 안성규 및 정효식, "사이버 전쟁 핵심 KCC 김정남이 설립 주도," 중앙일보, 2009년 7월 12일, http://nk.joins.com/news/view.asp?aid=3418751.
25. "북한의 사이버전 능력과 위협 전망," 군사논단, 제68호, 2011 년 겨울, 73쪽.
26. 윤규식, "북한의 사이버전 능력과 위협 전망," 군사논단, 제68호, 2011 년 겨울.
27. Alexandre Mansourov, "North Korea's Cyber Warfare and Challenges for the U.S.-ROK Alliance," Academic Paper Series, Korea Economic Institute of America, December 2, 2014, p 2; 임종인, 권유중, 장규현, 백승조, "북한의 사이버전력 현황과 한국의 국가적 대응전략," 국방정책연구, 제29권, 제4호, 2013 겨울, 21쪽; and Joseph S. Bermudez Jr., "SIGINT, EW, and EIW in the Korean People's Army: An Overview of Development and Organization," in *Bytes and Bullets: Information Technology Revolution and National Security on the Korean Peninsula*, ed. Alexandre Y. Mansourov (Honolulu: Asia-Pacific Center for Strategic Studies, 2005), 244–45.
28. 김흥광, "북한의 사이버테러정보전 능력과 사이버보안대책 제언," NK지식인연대, 2009.
29. 임종인, 권유중, 장규현, 백승조, "북한의 사이버전력 현황과 한국의 국가적 대응전략," 국방정책연구, 제29권, 제4호, 2013 겨울, 27쪽; 김인수 및 KMARMA (김건일, 박상구, 박은석, 박주호, 이상언, 림피팁), "북한 사이버전 수행능력의 평가와 전망," 통일정책연구, 제24권 1호, 2015, 131쪽.
30. Mansourov, "North Korea's Cyber Warfare," 4.
31. Ibid.
32. 김인수 및 KMARMA (김건일, 박상구, 박은석, 박주호, 이상언, 림피팁), "북한 사이버전 수행능력의 평가와 전망," 통일정책연구, 제24권 1호, 2015, 132쪽.
33. Valeriano and Maness place them in four categories: structured query language (SQL) for website defacement; distributed denial of service (DDoS); intrusions to include Trojans, trapdoors, or backdoors; and advanced persistent threats (APTs). Brandon Valeriano and Ryan C. Maness, *Cyber War Versus Cyber Realities: Cyber Conflict in the International System* (Oxford: Oxford University Press, 2015), 34–36.
34. Richard A. Clarke and Robert K. Knake, *Cyber War: The Next Threat to National Security and What to Do about It* (New York: Ecco, 2010), 12–16; Valeriano and Maness, *Cyber War Versus Cyber Realities*, 142–48; and P. W. Singer and Allan Friedman, *Cybersecurity and Cyberwar: What Everyone Needs to Know* (Oxford: Oxford University Press, 2014), 72–76.
35. The country is said to have a little over 1,000 IP addresses allotted. Martyn Williams, "North Korea Moves Quietly onto the Internet," *Computer World*, June 10, 2010; HP Security Research, "Profiling an Enigma"; and

Nicole Perlroth and David E. Sanger, "North Korea Loses Its Link to the Internet," *New York Times*, December 22, 2014.
36. 신창훈, "북한의 사이버 공격과 위협에 대한 우리의 대응," Issue Brief 2015-05, 아산정책연구원, 6 April 2015, 3쪽.
37. The U.S. DoD defines CNO as being "comprised of computer network attack, computer network defense, and related computer network exploitation enabling operations." *Department of Defense Dictionary of Military and Associated Terms*, Joint Chiefs of Staff, November 8, 2010 (as Amended through February 15, 2016).
38. Steve Sin, "Cyber Threat Posed by North Korea and China to South Korea and US Forces Korea," 2009 [translation of Korean text]; 신스티브, "한국과 주한미군에 대한 북한과 중국으로부터의 사이버 위협," 국방과 기술, Vol. 364, 2009년 6월.
39. *Department of Defense Dictionary of Military and Associated Terms.*
40. Jason Andress and Stee Winterfeld, *Cyber Warfare: Techniques, Tactics and Tools for Security Practitioners*, 2nd ed. (Waltham, MA: Syngress, 2014).
41. *Operation Blockbuster: Unraveling the Long Thread of the Sony Attack* (McLean, VA: Novetta, February 2016), https://www.operationblockbuster.com/wp-content/uploads/2016/02/Operation-Blockbuster-Report.pdf.
42. Ibid.
43. Ibid.
44. *Department of Defense Dictionary of Military and Associated Terms.*
45. 임종인, 권유중, 장규현, 백승조, "북한의 사이버전력 현황과 한국의 국가적 대응전략," 국방정책연구, 제29권 제4호, 2013년 겨울, 22쪽.
46. 허광섭, "오늘의 사회주의수호전은 사회생활의 모든 분야에서 제국주의를 압도하기 위한 투쟁," 김일성종합대학학보 (철학, 경제), 주체103 (2014)년 제60권 제3호.
47. Daniel A. Pinkston, "North and South Korean Views of the U.S.-Japan Alliance," in *The US-Japan Alliance: Balancing Soft and Hard Power in East Asia*, ed. Tsuneo Akaha and David Arase (New York: Routledge, 2011).
48. Article 7 of the National Security Act, promulgated in 1948 and subsequently revised, prohibits the "import, reproduction, possession, carrying, distribution, selling or acquisition of any documents, drawings or other expression materials, with the intention of supporting anti-government organization." The act serves as the legal foundation for South Korea's censorship of pro–North Korean websites. "National Security Act," full text available at http://www.law.go.kr/eng/engMain.do.
49. 이상호, "소셜미디어(SNS)기반 사이버 심리전 공격 실태 및 대응방향," 국가정보연구, 제5권 2호, 2013년 7월.
50. "북한사이버테러, 최근 해외 160여 웹사이트 외 SNS 대남심리전 강화," 블루투데이 (BlueToday.net), 2015년 4월 30일, http://www.bluetoday.net/news/articleView.html?idxno=8815.
51. "한국 국민, 北 사이버 심리전에 노출돼 있어," *Daily NK*, 2015년 4원 13일.
52. John Markoff, "Old Trick Threatens the Newest Weapons," *New York Times*, October 26, 2009; and William J. Broad, John Markoff, and David E. Sanger, "Israeli Test on Worm Called Crucial in Iran Nuclear Delay," *New York Times*, January 15, 2011.
53. 윤규식, "북한의 사이버전 능력과 위협 전망," 군사논단, 제68호, 2011 년 겨울, 75쪽
54. 河周希, "〔집중해부〕 핵무기 개발하는 북한 제2자연과학원의 실체," 月刊朝鮮, 2013년 5월호.
55. 송홍근, "잠수함 美 본토 접근해 핵 공격 남조선 타격은 '주체포'로 충분," 신동아, 2015년 2월 7일.
56. Other prestigious institutions of higher education that produce IT and computer specialists include Kim Chaek University of Technology and Pyongyang Computer Technology University.
57. "College of Computer Science," Kim Il-sung University website, October 31, 2014, http://www.ryongnamsan.edu.kp/univ/success/depart/11; and "Faculty of Electronics and Au-

tomation," Kim Il-sung University website, October 31, 2014, http://www.ryongnamsan.edu.kp/univ/success/depart/18.

58. "Information Technology Institute," Kim Il-sung University website, October 31, 2014, http://www.ryongnamsan.edu.kp/univ/success/institute/27.
59. 윤규식, "북한의 사이버전 능력과 위협 전망," 군사논단, 제68호, 2011 년 겨울, 75-76쪽.
60. 박근태, "북한, 돈 못버는 'IT사령부' 해체," 한국경제신문, 2015년 11월 11일.
61. 통일부, "조선컴퓨터센터," 북한정보포털, http://nkinfo.unikorea.go.kr/.
62. Joseph S. Bermudez Jr., "38 North Special Report: A New Emphasis on Operations against South Korea?" *38 North*, Special Report 4, June 11, 2010.
63. 윤규식, "북한의 사이버전 능력과 위협 전망," 군사논단, 제68호, 2011 년 겨울, 77쪽.
64. 정재욱, "'남한의 선거에 개입' 지시한 김정은," 미래한국, 2016년 3월 22일.
65. Ibid.
66. 유동열, "베일에 감춰진 美 제재 대상," 주간조선, 2340호, 2015년 1월 12일.
67. Ibid.; and "Treasury Imposes Sanctions against the Government of the Democratic People's Republic of Korea," U.S. Department of the Treasury, January 2, 2015, https://www.treasury.gov/press-center/press-releases/Pages/jl9733.aspx.
68. 정재욱, "'남한의 선거에 개입' 지시한 김정은," 미래한국, 2016년 3월 22일.
69. 유동열, "베일에 감춰진 美 제재 대상," 주간조선, 2340호, 2015년 1월 12일.
70. 전수일, "북 사이버부대 실태 알리는 김흥광 대표," RFA, January 26, 2015, http://www.rfa.org/korean/weekly_program/rfa_interview/rfainterview-01262015095622.html; and HP Security Research, "Profiling an Enigma."
71. Valeriano and Maness, *Cyber War Versus Cyber Realities*.
72. Stephan Haggard and Jon R. Lindsay, "North Korea and the Sony Hack: Exporting Instability through Cyberspace," *Asia Pacific Issues*, no. 115 (May 2015).
73. Ibid.
74. Tobias Feakin, "Playing Blind-Man's Buff: Estimating North Korea's Cyber Capabilities," *International Journal of Korean Unification Studies* 22, no. 2 (2013): 63–90; and Intel Security Inc., "Dissecting Operation Troy: Cyberespionage in South Korea," McAfee Labs Blog, July 8, 2013, https://blogs.mcafee.com/mcafee-labs/dissecting-operation-troy-cyberespionage-in-south-korea/.
75. "[3·20 사이버 테러] 최근 주요 사이버 테러 6건 모두 北 소행," 조선일보, 2013년 3월 21일, http://news.chosun.com/site/data/html_dir/2013/03/21/2013032100223.html.
76. Ibid.; and "Ten Days of Rain," McAfee White Paper, 2011, http://www.mcafee.com/us/resources/white-papers/wp-10-days-of-rain.pdf.
77. "[3·20 사이버 테러] 최근 주요 사이버 테러 6건 모두 北 소행," 조선일보, 2013년 3월 21일, http://news.chosun.com/site/data/html_dir/2013/03/21/2013032100223.html.
78. Feakin, "Playing Blind-Man's Buff."
79. Haggard and Lindsay, "North Korea and the Sony Hack"; Federal Bureau of Investigation, "Update on Sony Investigation," press release, Washington, DC, December 19, 2014; and *Operation Blockbuster*.
80. Caroline Baylon with Roger Brunt and David Livingstone, "Cyber Security at Civil Nuclear Facilities: Understanding the Risks," Chatham House Report, September 2015; James Conca, "Hacking of South Korean Nuclear Reactors Poses No Danger," *Forbes*, December 24, 2014, http://www.forbes.com/sites/jamesconca/2014/12/24/hacking-of-south-korean-nuclear-reactors-poses-no-danger/; and Ju-Min Park and Meeyoung Cho, "South Korea Blames North Korea for December Hack on Nuclear Operator," Reuters, March 17, 2015, http://www.reuters.com/article/us-nuclear-southkorea-northkorea-idUSKBN0MD0GR20150317.
81. For a skeptical view, see Soo-Kyung Koo, "Cyber Security in South Korea: The Threat Within," *Diplomat*, August 19, 2013.
82. European Network and Information Security Agency (ENISA), "National Cyber Security

Strategies: An Implementation Guide," December 19, 2012, 2, https://www.enisa.europa.eu/publications/national-cyber-security-strategies-an-implementation-guide.

83. Korea Internet and Security Agency (KISA), "2015 Korea Internet White Paper," October 16, 2015, 81–84; and Hyeong-Wook Boo and Kang-Kyu Lee, "Cyber War and Policy Suggestions for South Korean Planners," *International Journal of Korean Unification Studies* 21, no. 2 (2012): 94–95.
84. For a brief review of international relations theories and views of cyberspace and cyber war in the context of the Korean peninsula, see Hyeong-Wook Boo and Kang-Kyu Lee, "Cyber War and Policy Suggestions."
85. Yunsik Jake Jang and Bo Young Lim, "Harmonization among National Cyber Security and Cybercrime Response Organizations: New Challenges of Cybercrime," working paper, 2013, http://arxiv.org/pdf/1308.2362v1.
86. This trend is apparent in the content of a South Korean draft cyberterrorism bill that was released on February 22, 2016. The bill is sponsored by twenty-four National Assembly lawmakers but fails to address the need to differentiate among espionage, crime, vandalism, sabotage, terrorism, the use of force, and armed attack in cyberspace. These distinctions are important for formulating appropriate responses, but the draft bill refers to almost all cyber operations as "cyber terror." "국가 사이버테러 방지 등에 관한 법률안," 의안번호 18583, 2016 년 2월 22 일. See Michael M. Schmitt, ed., *Tallinn Manual on the International Law Applicable to Cyber Warfare* (Cambridge: Cambridge University Press, 2013).
87. ROK government, "National Cyber Security Masterplan," August 2, 2011.
88. MSIP, "한-미,AI기반 사이버보안기술 공동 개발 추진," 보도자료, 2016년 5월 3 일.
89. The five levels are: normal; concern; caution; warning; severe (정상; 관심; 주의; 경계; 심각). The level was raised to "concern" on January 8, 2016, and to "caution" on February 11, 2016. MSIP, "민간분야 사이버공격 대비 공동모의훈련 실시," 보도자료, 2016년 2월 25 일; MSIP, "미래부, 국방부와 사이버안보 공조 대응태세 강화," 보도자료, 2016년 4월 6 일.
90. Available on the APCERT website, http://www.apcert.org/.
91. "Microsoft Launches Korea Cybersecurity Center Advancing Fight against Cyberthreats," Microsoft Asia News Center, March 4, 2016, https://news.microsoft.com/apac/2016/03/04/microsoft-launches-korea-cybersecurity-center-advancing-fight-against-cyberthreats; MSIP, "미래부-마이크로소프트社, 사이버보안 공조 강화," 보도자료, 2016년 3월 5 일.
92. For example, the Stuxnet worm spread to other industrial systems in other systems in other countries even though it was designed specifically to infect uranium-enrichment centrifuges in Iran.
93. Boris Kondoch, "Jus ad Bellum and Cyber Warfare in Northeast Asia," *Journal of East Asia and International Law* 6, no. 2 (2013).
94. Cordula Droege, "Get off My Cloud; Cyber Warfare, International Humanitarian Law, and the Protection of Civilians," *International Review of the Red Cross* 94, no. 886 (Summer 2012).
95. Michael M. Schmitt, "'Below the Threshold' Cyber Operations: The Countermeasures Response Option and International Law," *Virginia Journal of International Law* 54, no. 3 (2013).
96. During June and July 1950, the UN Security Council adopted four resolutions related to the Korean War. The resolutions were adopted during a Soviet boycott in protest to support the People's Republic of China replacing the Republic of China as a permanent member of the Security Council. Resolution 83 recommended that UN member states assist the Republic of Korea to repel the armed attack from the North. Resolution 84 recommended states providing military assistance to make their forces available to a unified command [United Nations Command] under the United States. The resolution also asked the United States to name the commander and authorized the use of the UN flag. Sixteen countries, or

"sending states," sent military forces to assist the Republic of Korea during the war. Some of these states still participate in UNC activities and exercises. UN Security Council Resolution 83 (adopted June 27, 1950), available at http://www.un.org/en/ga/search/view_doc.asp?symbol=S/RES/83(1950); UN Security Council Resolution 84 (adopted July 7, 1950), https://documents-dds-ny.un.org/doc/RESOLUTION/GEN/NR0/064/97/IMG/NR006497.pdf; and "United Nations Command," US Forces Korea website, http://www.usfk.mil/About/United-Nations-Command/.

Safety & Security

A Three-Layer Framework for a Comprehensive National Cybersecurity Strategy

Eviatar Matania, Lior Yoffe, and Michael Mashkautsan

The growing impact of cyberspace on practically every aspect of our personal and collective lives is no longer a question. Enabling free flow of knowledge, capital, and services with low entry barriers, it improves social welfare and encourages innovation. The reliance of many traditional activities on cyberspace is ever increasing, while new important activities therein regularly emerge. As a result and given its extensive influence on the activities of individuals, organizations, societies, and economies, cyberspace has gained immense strategic importance.

At the same time, the risks emanating from it have also been rapidly rising, transforming into a completely new type of threat. From initially only endangering information assets, the cyber threat is now a comprehensive risk to all of the organization's systems—management, services, operations, security, and others. Once the exclusive worry of information security officers, it is fiercely drawing the attention of executives worldwide as one of the major risks to their organizations.

Furthermore, cybersecurity has long ceased to be merely a problem of organizations. In recent years it has been globally acknowledged as a tangible threat to numerous national security interests, such as disruption of essential processes, services, and infrastructure; harm to human lives; or systemic failure of national consequence, thereby emerging as a key priority for policymakers.

This realization has led many countries to initiate policy processes aimed at identifying cyber threats to their national interests and developing a preliminary national approach to handle them. However, since cyberspace is a highly technological domain, bearing little resemblance to other national security domains we have grown to understand, many policymakers may be challenged in framing the problem through familiar terms and may even lack the basic intuition to adequately assess and manage these risks.

A major obstacle in this regard is current taxonomy. Its first type analyzes cyber threats from an organizational or network standpoint, mainly focusing on either the technical level (e.g., the NIST frameworks[1]) or risk assessment processes (e.g., Defense-in-Depth and Intelligence-Driven Defense[2]). Its second type handles cyber threats through the prism of national security and public policy by trying to incorporate them in existing terminology borrowed from strategic military concepts (e.g., Technology-Driven RMA[3]), parallels in international law, or others. Both types fail to adequately

Eviatar Matania has been head of the Israel National Cyber Bureau (INCB) since its establishment on January 1, 2012.

Lior Yoffe is head of defense planning in the INCB and a PhD candidate in Tel Aviv University in the field of cybersecurity.

Michael Mashkautsan is chief of staff in the INCB.

support policymakers in addressing the issue, as most of them come from fundamentally different backgrounds.

Therefore, there is growing necessity for a dedicated taxonomy stemming from a comprehensive national perspective and inherently reflecting the goals, roles, and efforts of the government in cybersecurity. Moreover, there is an increasing need for a systematic approach to the analysis of this relatively new challenge in order to enable the development of a comprehensive national cybersecurity strategy.

The objective of this paper is to address this need by proposing a generic framework—the result of extensive study of national security strategic thinking fused with cybersecurity research. It also reflects lessons learned during the last three years in leading countries that embarked on this demanding endeavor, with an emphasis on the specific insights and practical experience obtained in Israel through its own journey in cyberspace.

This paper aims to support policymakers on the sectoral, national, and international levels, as well as researchers in academia and industry who are grappling with the crucial, albeit daunting, task of boosting cybersecurity. The paper starts by presenting the special role of organizations as the elementary units of the national cyber domain. It continues with introducing the three layers of the proposed framework—robustness, resilience, and defense—succeeded by a comprehensive analysis of the interconnections between them and a concluding remark on general aspects in the deployment of the proposed framework.

Organizations as the Primary Subjects of a National Cybersecurity Strategy

We begin with three fundamental characteristics of cyberspace, which underlie the crucial part of organizations as they form the key medium for the propagation and realization of cyber threats.

First, cyberspace is a man-made domain of computerized systems, networks, and their interconnections—each of them ultimately owned and operated by a defined organization. There are barely any no-man's-lands and almost no international territories in cyberspace. Second, cyber threats all but ignore national borders as they take advantage of interconnectivity to target organizations directly. To date there is no sufficient solution, technological or operational, that can comprehensively differentiate between "good" and "bad" communications in cyberspace, to stop malicious activity therein from crossing national borders. Moreover, as cyberspace quickly expands and the complexity of its topology continuously rises, hopes of devising such a solution are gradually diminishing. Third, cybersecurity is inextricable from the organization's functioning. For an organization to guarantee the proper execution of its mission, it has to manage its cybersecurity in sync with all of its other operational considerations and efforts, thereby making network defense an inseparable part, in responsibility as in implementation, of its holistic network and operations management.

The combination of these three characteristics leads us to the fundamental conclusion that organizations essentially constitute the nation's digital frontier, and as such, they must be the primary subjects of any national cybersecurity framework.

This is a central, crucial, and nontrivial observation. National security has traditionally focused on territory or people as primary subjects of interest. Even the basic terms of "sovereignty" and "jurisdiction" are mostly defined with regard to territory or population. Hence, the notion that efforts and resources should be first invested in organizations, which are in many ways merely virtual entities, is quite unprecedented in national security. We maintain that this understanding is vital for any decision making in the realm of national cybersecurity, and its logic stands at the heart of the proposed framework.

Layer 1: Robustness

The first layer of the proposed framework is the systemic capacity to repel and contain cyber threats. We refer to this capacity as robustness, formally defined as being capable of performing without failure under a wide range of conditions. Yet, systemic robustness can hardly be achieved without the robustness of the elementary units at risk. Since organizations are the elementary units of the national cyber domain, national cyber robustness is primarily based on the cyber robustness of organizations, meaning their continuous readiness to deny and mitigate threats by themselves.

The human body offers an instructive example of robustness at the level of the elementary unit, as it can impressively withstand on its own substantial shifts in its environment: in temperature, oxygen, moisture, sunlight, nutrition, strain, etc. That can be considered as individual health robustness. Proceeding to the state level, beyond the responsibility of every citizen to their and their children's health, national health robustness heavily relies on state actions that systematically enhance individual health robustness, such as educating for personal hygiene, providing sanitation and clean water, issuing vaccinations, and so forth.

A similar approach could be applied to cybersecurity. At the level of the elementary unit, namely, the organizational level, cybersecurity measures that promote robustness can be classified into several main efforts, among them (1) organizational processes, foremost of which is risk assessment that establishes a baseline for periodic work plans, adequate allocation of resources, and procurement policy; (2) technical steps that reduce the probability of a successful attack or of substantial damage, such as network segmentation, user privilege policy, access control, data encryption, and authentication mechanisms; and (3) procedures focused on the human factor that narrow accidental or malicious errors from within, through awareness, classification, and training of employees.[4] Other efforts that contribute to organizational robustness may include penetration tests or secured development of the organization or its suppliers.

Advancing to the national level, state actions to enhance organizations' robustness may vary considerably depending on the legal ecosystem, corporate norms, and other attributes of the country in question. We list three prevalent categories: (1) raising the awareness of target audiences, namely, management and stakeholders, to risks and mitigation;[5] (2) setting and adjusting cybersecurity standards and raising the bar for cybersecurity in prioritized areas (e.g., professional workforce and services, products and acquisition, continuous situational awareness processes) through dissemination of best practices, setup of designated incentives, sector-specific requirements, and regulation of the various cybersecurity providers; (3) promoting national preparedness through exercises, disaster recovery plans, and standard procedures to anticipate and handle a serious attack or breach.

It should be clear that the nature of the governmental measures to encourage organizations to take action to improve their robustness will vary among sectors and organizations, prioritized on the basis of a periodic holistic assessment. The criteria for such a process will generally involve the probability of disruption of essential processes, services, and infrastructure (e.g., provision of water and electricity, banking and health care, communications, respectively); harm to human lives (e.g., transportation and chemicals); or immense aggregate damage through systemic failure across a region or a sector (e.g., through vast IP or data theft). As a result, some sectors and organizations, whose breach would potentially be of national consequence, may require substantially deeper and tougher government intervention and regulation.

To summarize, the first layer of the proposed framework—robustness—addresses the systemic capacity to repel and contain threats in the national cyber domain through its elementary units: the organizations.

Layer 2: Resilience

Still, organizational robustness has its limits. Since it essentially relies on a set of mechanisms and technological procedures defined by risk management considerations, it is relatively static. That does not imply inflexibility but rather transformation timescales that substantially lag behind the rapid dynamics of cyber threats. In addition, robustness is inherently disconnected from the constant cyber events outside the organization, even if they may clearly have a bearing on its security.

Therefore, there is a need for an event-driven, complementary effort to handle cyber incidents and to stop their proliferation. This task is aggravated by the comparative ease in duplicating attacks in a hyper-connected cyberspace and the fact that instances of so many vulnerable systems are shared by numerous organizations. Thus, the second layer of the proposed framework is the systemic capacity to handle threats, when they inevitably materialize, in order to regain overall normal functioning as soon as possible. We refer to this capacity as resilience, formally defined as the ability to recover from or adjust easily to misfortune or change.

Following the previous example, the resilience of the health-care system is determined by its ability to handle medical consequences of different events. Even when the public is aware, hygienic, and vaccinated, people get sick or injured. There is only so much the human body can manage without external help, and so HMOs and hospitals provide a second tier of recovery through tailored personal treatment. On the national and global levels, when individual cases indicate a possible outbreak of a contagious disease, institutes like the Centers for Disease Control and Prevention (CDC) step in to provide the third tier of resilience through sharing information, dispatching special research teams, instructing the public, and more.

In the cyber context, organizational resilience implies the capability to detect threats, prevent their infiltration or at least confine their expansion, manage their effects, and deny their recurrence. The past two decades have seen the development of myriad products and services that enable such organizational preparedness. For instance, antivirus companies seek to prevent known or semi-known threats from exploiting additional systems after being discovered and identified.

However, beyond the extensive work conducted by the private sector, governments have a major role in establishing a national mitigation capacity. On top of the nearly exclusive capabilities they muster in investigation, intelligence, and analysis, only governments can resolve market failures that stem from lack of trust, joint infrastructures, or substantial investments in hubs of unique expertise.

According to our analysis and experience, the following are the main governmental efforts to improve national resilience, many of which can and should be implemented in cooperation with the industry: (1) creating situational awareness of events and indications, which enables the identification of linked phenomena and intelligent prioritization of work; (2) establishing profound analytic capacity, which enables thorough understanding for effective mitigation; (3) facilitating a secured information-sharing mechanism and distributing actionable intelligence; (4) handling incidents and assisting in proactively denying the attack or recovering from it, usually hand in hand with the private organizations at risk or operating the compromised component.

The most common embodiment of these is the national Computer Security Incident Response Team (CSIRT). Many countries have been establishing national CSIRTs during the past few years with varying mandates, usually aiming to enhance public-private partnership by facilitating information sharing to better mitigate cyber incidents. The European Union, for example, determined that member states should establish a well-functioning network of CSIRTs in order to respond to online security breaches in real-time conditions.[6]

To summarize, the resilience layer covers the event-driven actions that should be taken by organizations and the state, separately or together, to identify, mitigate, and recover from cyber attacks, so as to minimize potential damages and maintain systemic continuity as long as possible.

Layer 3: Defense

Established properly, robustness and resilience should handle most cyber attacks from low to medium complexity. Yet there is a key element of the cyber threat that has so far been overlooked, which fundamentally distinguishes it from its health-care analogue—the existence of a human perpetrator with malicious intent. This fact is manifested in two ways. First, cyber aggressors can adaptively interact with their targets over long time frames, meticulously studying their defenses in order to circumvent or outsmart them. Second, even if an attack is detected, an organization, other than to stop or manipulate it, has no authority, and usually no capability, to engage its perpetrator in a manner that will deny future attempts. It can only try to better prepare for the next round. And so, when considering persistent cyber attackers with high-end expertise and adequate resources, even a high level of preparedness and event-driven capacity are not enough.

Accordingly, the third layer of the proposed framework is defense, namely, the capacity to disrupt cyber attacks by focusing on the human factor behind them through national operational defense capabilities. These can only be developed and executed by the government and are tightly linked to its unique authority to act against criminals and adversaries. Focused on attackers and campaigns, these capabilities comprise various elements, many of which are familiar from other areas of national security: early warning systems and processes, a developed legal framework with suitable law enforcement capacity, proactive means to deter and defeat foreign threats and so on.[7]

The defense layer consists of two main vectors for handling attackers. The first focuses on criminal entities through national and international mechanisms of law enforcement, mainly police forces and justice systems. The Council of Europe's Convention on Cybercrime (the Budapest Convention) is an instructive example, as it works to align national legislation of its members and to establish collaborative processes that support prosecution of criminal elements. The second vector concentrates on adversaries of the state looking to harm national interests, be it terror organizations or other countries. This effort is tightly linked with other actions, taken by defense and intelligence establishments, which identify cyberspace as an evolving warfare domain necessitating adequate weapons, intelligence gathering capabilities, and deterrence capacity.

However, adhering to the traditional distinctions among crime, terror, and state actors may prove to be troublesome in cyberspace for several reasons. First, certain states are constantly and increasingly working through criminal or terror proxies to cover their tracks. In addition, some criminal attacks may be of national consequence, IP thefts serving as a leading example of late. Finally, the flow of know-how and capabilities among all these actors appears to be practically unstoppable, if not continuously rising. Moreover, even when perpetrators are identified, that usually happens long after decisions have to be made with regard to handling the event, so that formal jurisdiction can often be determined only in retrospect. As a result, developing effective operational national defense capabilities requires a new approach to mechanisms that enable quick and flexible interaction and synchronization between the traditional related government agencies, sometimes through the establishment of designated bodies, as in the case of the United States and Israel.[8]

Analysis of Interconnections among the Three Layers

The three layers notably differ in two fundamental aspects. First is their focus. The robustness and resilience layers focus on attacks, before, during, or after their occurrence, resembling in many ways the familiar efforts of civil defense, with the former aiming toward general offline preparedness for a wide range of threats, while the latter is set on handling specific events. The defense layer, on the other hand, focuses on attackers and campaigns with a similar perspective to that of security and intelligence establishments. Second is where the central role for implementation lies. In the first layer, organizations are obviously the main change agents, with the state playing an incentivizing and supporting role. In the second layer, organizations and the state must collaborate to successfully leverage local and national assets and capabilities. In the third layer, the government has a practically exclusive mandate based on its unique authority to act against criminals and adversaries.

It should be emphasized that the three layers are mutually dependent and complementary by structure, meaning they cannot replace one another. Robustness is necessary for sustainable resilience, as the ability to repel the majority of threats allows the effective mitigation of those that do materialize. Resilience enables defense, as the ability to handle events allows the resolved allocation of attention and resources to disrupt the attackers and plays a part in their effective deterrence. Hence follows the importance of gradual and combined national progress in all three layers.

Finally, there is an ongoing process of improvement at all layers, as every attack, successful or not, can be analyzed to adapt and enhance the structures of robustness (e.g., through a different threat reference, standardization mechanisms, or incentivization techniques), resilience (e.g., through alternative early warning systems and policies, information-sharing platforms, or recovery processes) and defense (e.g., through deeper understanding of attackers' interests, strategies, and methods). Of particular importance is the flow of information and feedback among the three layers, as it allows

Essence of the Three Layers

	Layer 1: Robustness	Layer 2: Resilience	Layer 3: Defense
Focus	Attacks	Attacks	Attackers and campaigns
Context	Offline	Event driven	Attacker driven
Organizations	Execute	Execute	—
Government	Incentivizes and regulates	Execute	Execute

their coherent development and truly holistic national cybersecurity, which substantially exceeds the mere combination of the three layers.

Deployment

The proposed framework described is fundamental and independent of specific deployment, which can take different forms. Nevertheless, it is worth mentioning three of the general aspects that should affect any deployment outline, regardless of the country in question, its political system, its regulatory environment, and its current operational capabilities.

First, public-private partnerships are a necessity, owing to the aforementioned role of organizations and the fact that a great share of the advanced knowledge and skills lies with the private sector. Second, the timescales characteristic of governmental bureaucracy and buildup of operational capabilities tend to lag far behind those of cyber threats and technologies. Smartphones, cloud computing, and the Internet of Things are but a few examples of evolutions that are constantly and dramatically changing the way organizations and people do business. To stay on top of current and future threats, any sustainable governmental deployment requires substantial agility in authority and resources. Third, there is a need to implement the three layers in a structure that coherently binds them in order to support their mutual feedback. This feedback process is a key pillar in a comprehensive national cybersecurity scheme.

Conclusion

The rapid evolution of cyberspace has turned the old known field of information security into a new risk to national security interests and has led states to start investing effort, budgets, and thinking in facing this new threat. The first step toward a well-defined response is the development of a comprehensive national cybersecurity strategy.

Building on the combination of research, system analysis, and practical experience, this paper suggests a generic framework to this endeavor based on three layers: robustness (the systemic capacity to repel and contain most cyber threats), resilience (the systemic capacity to handle threats when they inevitably materialize), and defense (the capacity to disrupt cyber attacks by focusing on the human factor behind them).

The three layers are complementary and mutually dependent. Established robustness allows the effective handling of cyber events, meaning resilience, which in turn allows the resolved effort to disrupt and deter the attackers, meaning defense. Thus, a proper national strategy should address all three layers concurrently.

The taxonomy and framework presented in this paper can be instructive in identifying and differentiating the responsibility, mission, authority, capabilities, and resources of each player on the national level and may thereby support policymakers as they lead the formulation and adaptation of national cyber security strategies in the coming years.

Notes

1. The National Institute of Standards and Technology.
2. E. M. Hutchins, M. J. Cloppert, and R. M. Amin, "Intelligence-Driven Computer Network Defense Informed by Analysis of Adversary Campaigns and Intrusion Kill Chains," *Leading Issues in Information Warfare & Security Research* 1 (2011): 80.
3. Revolution in Military Affairs.
4. Standards, certifications, and best practices are a good example of a method to enhance robustness. Specifically, the ISO 27XXX series is a growing family of international standards designed to improve robustness in information technology systems and techniques.
5. The Australian Communications and Media Authority (ACMA) published an overview of international cybersecurity awareness raising and educational initiatives, offering a significant comparative analysis of such campaigns in several countries: www.acma.gov.au/webwr/_assets/main/lib310665/galexia_report-overview_intnl_cybersecurity_awareness.pdf.
6. "Europe 2020 Strategy: A Digital Single Market, Pillar III: Trust & Security." European Commission website, https://ec.europa.eu/digital-single-market/en/our-goals/pillar-iii-trust-security.
7. For example, the United Kingdom stated in its cybersecurity strategy that "the government will continue to build up in GCHQ and MOD our sovereign UK capability to detect and defeat high-end threats." *The UK Cyber Security Strategy: Protecting and Promoting the UK in a Digital World*, Information Policy Team, Cabinet Office, November 2011, www.gov.uk/government/uploads/system/uploads/attachment_data/file/60961/uk-cyber-security-strategy-final.pdf.
8. White House, "Establishment of the Cyber Threat Intelligence Integration Center," U.S. Presidential Memorandum, February 25, 2015, https://www.whitehouse.gov/the-press-office/2015/02/25/presidential-memorandum-establishment-cyber-threat-intelligence-integrat; Establishment of the National Cyber Security Authority, Resolution No. 2444 of the Government of Israel on "Advancing the National Preparedness for Cyber Security," February 15, 2015.

The Cybersecurity Storm Front—Forces Shaping the Cybersecurity Landscape

A Framework for Analysis

Samuel Sanders Visner

The managing and shaping of the offerings for a cybersecurity business and the teaching of an undergraduate course on cybersecurity policy, operations, and technology present a dual challenge. This challenge imposes the need to understand what is happening on the cybersecurity landscape, how the forces shaping that landscape relate to each other, and how governments and other enterprises should respond to those forces. This challenge has also impelled the author to attempt to describe to students these forces in a coherent fashion.

The media focuses on the dramatic consequences of recent cybersecurity breaches (e.g., Sony, Anthem, the U.S. government's Office of Personnel Management, and other incidents). At the same time, our understanding of the cybersecurity landscape is often fragmented, which the cybersecurity industry and its practitioners fail to relate. For example, why are our information technology (IT) infrastructures continuing to demonstrate significant vulnerability? Are the steps we might take to reduce that vulnerability likely to remain effective as these infrastructures change? If we do a more complete job of sharing threat intelligence, what privacy implications must we face? Are the breaches with which we're contending "merely" the result of cyber crime, or are we seeing emerge a new component of statecraft, one that must become part of our international relations calculus? The speed with we must address these questions and the changes associated with some of the underlying factors calls for a more coherent cybersecurity framework. We need a framework that allows us to analyze events and develop courses of action within an ever-changing cybersecurity environment. Because these factors are changing so rapidly and simultaneously, the term "cybersecurity storm front"—a turbulent place that changes rapidly, with potentially disruptive consequences for those over whom the storm front passes—applies. While the term "storm front" may appear hyperbolic, the need to improve analysis and generate more useful hypotheses deserves as much attention as the cybersecurity profession can allow, and it is to the confluence of these forces that the paper refers, and not necessarily to the effects of any specific cybersecurity event. This article discusses five prominent factors shaping this storm front:

1. the growing importance of the information managed by increasingly complex IT infrastructures,
2. the technology and structure of the IT infrastructures we seek to safeguard,

Samuel Sanders Visner is senior vice president and general manager at Enterprise Cybersecurity and Resilience, ICF International, and an adjunct professor of cybersecurity at the Science and Technology in International Affairs Program at the Edmund A. Walsh School of Foreign Service at Georgetown University. He previously served as vice president and general manager of the Computer Sciences Corporation Cybersecurity and chief of the Signals Intelligence Programs at the National Security Agency.

3. the changing technological and operational nature of the threat that jeopardizes those infrastructures and the information they manage,

4. the changing role of cybersecurity as an instrument of statecraft, and

5. the changing privacy relationship of citizens to the enterprises that employ complex IT infrastructures.

Taken together, these factors can be used to analyze cybersecurity developments, identify and analyze the consequences of these developments, and hopefully, aid the development of policies, doctrines, and resources to help us manage these consequences.

What We Must Protect

Well documented and broadly discussed in policy and current cybersecurity literature are both the various domains we seek to protect in the United States and elsewhere and the domains subject to exploitation (stealing of information) and attack (damage to information, information systems, and the infrastructures that depend on information). In brief, in the United States, these domains are described by the Comprehensive National Cybersecurity Initiative (CNCI), signed by former president Bush in 2006 and supported by President Obama. CNCI defined those domains in which cybersecurity disciplines are exercised as .gov, .mil, companies comprising the defense industrial base, owners and operators of critical infrastructure, and certain key manufacturers.[1] A number of CNCI initiatives followed, as well as a series of presidential executive orders (EOs). Most notable was EO 13636, which named the sectors of critical infrastructure, sectors the cybersecurity of which represent a significant public interest.[2]

Important to understand and consider are the cybersecurity consequences of changes in the IT on which government, military, the defense industrial base, critical infrastructures, and other enterprises depend. These changes are far-reaching. Defending the enterprises that depend on them presents new challenges because these technologies are shaping infrastructures more complex and more dynamic than those that preceded them.

The Rising Importance of Information

The role of information within enterprises is changing, growing more important, and helping shape our view of cybersecurity. The importance of information can be viewed as an enterprise's "information intensity." In the general economy, information—and by extension, its security—is recognized as an essential aspect of corporate strategy and, more important, as an enterprise's overarching value proposition. The concept of information intensity reflects the recognized value of information. This concept has existed for decades but gained currency in the 1980s and has experienced rising importance through the present day. Two types of information intensity were defined in the 1980s, and both are vital to today's enterprise: *product information intensity* and *value chain information intensity*.[3]

Product information intensity measures the extent to which a product is information-based (i.e., information-as-product), which is increasingly the case in today's global economy in general and in the United States and other advanced economies in particular. Any business that provides information-for-value (e.g., financial reporting and transactions, media, and social networking) delivers one or more products that make up principally (or solely) information. For such enterprises, the security of the information they employ and provide affects materially the value of the product they convey to their customers. Their value proposition can exist and thrive only to the extent cybersecurity and information assurance (relating to provenance, processing, and delivery) are present.

Value chain information intensity describes the extent to which information contributes to the production and delivery of noninformation products. Global supply chains for the manufacture of aircraft, for example, rely on a complex web of information ranging from specifications and test data to pricing and delivery schedules. Every element of this information is crucial to production. In fact, many of the processes used in manufacturing are IT controlled, enhancing the level of information intensity on which these products and their value chains rely. Cybersecurity failure in these value chains can result in faulty parts, dangerous industrial operations, loss of intellectual property, and nondelivery of the product as promised.

Linked to value-chain intensity is the extent to which many physical products (e.g., airliners) are characterized by an increasing proportion of information technologies. Today's Boeing Dreamliner, for example, uses computer-based "fly-by-wire" technologies to control critical flight systems. It possesses Internet-based architectures for other systems ranging from avionics to passenger entertainment subsystems. In many ways, the Dreamliner is a computer around which someone designed an airplane. In Boeing's own parlance, "The 787 Dreamliner, the world's first e-Enabled commercial airplane, combines the power of integrated information and communications systems to drive operational efficiency, enhance revenue, and streamline airplane maintenance."[4]

Boeing also notes,

> These tools promise to change the flow of information and create a new level of situational awareness that airlines can use to improve operations. At the same time, the extensive e-Enabling on the 787 increases the need for network connectivity, hardware and software improvements, and systems management practices.[5]

The importance of the concept of information intensity is not new. Compelling work by Michael E. Porter and Victor A. Miller in 1985 described the value of information in both information-as-product and value chains.[6] The authors defined the concept of manufacturing information and distribution systems (MIDS), noting that "an information intensive MIDS will generally bring value to a company if it adds high value to the product."[7] In today's world, such systems are of vital importance.

Whether an enterprise delivers information itself as a product or products that rely on information to empower and mediate their value chains, cybersecurity clearly bears directly on information intensity and on corporate strategy and the value proposition an enterprise delivers. Indeed, the cybersecurity of information-intensive products is intrinsic to the value of those products and rises, therefore, to the level of a corporate strategic issue.

Recent research makes even more important the concept of information intensity and more urgent the focus on cybersecurity. For example, this research provides powerful evidence about information-intensive businesses that produce information-as-product: These businesses should use information technology to disaggregate their production for the purpose of efficiency, just as value-chain information-intensive manufacturers are building global IT-enabled value and production chains.[8] Such disaggregation is an important component of corporate strategy designed to take advantage of regional and local specialization and cost structures.

At the same time, securing the IT infrastructures involved is essential for every aspect of development, production, integration, and delivery. Indeed, in all of these cases, the ability to provide effective cybersecurity is an essential enabling element of strategy. It can even be a competitive discriminator vis-á-vis competitors for which product quality (e.g., provenance and test data) and the integrity of information can be enhanced by cybersecurity.

The publication of Porter and Miller's work came, perhaps, too early for the application of the term "big data" used frequently today. Had the term been in vogue, Porter and Miller might have added *information analysis value.*

This term describes the ability of today's analytic tools to aggregate data from many sources (and of many types, i.e., heterogeneous data) in a homogeneous environment to create decisions of significant value. Some examples are what products to offer specific consumers at specific prices and times, how to deploy valuable medical research and development resources, what crop futures the market might expect, or the likely progression of a dangerous epidemic. Tools applied from disciplines such as "business intelligence," "enterprise resource management," and "data mining" amplify considerably the value of information.

Overall, no surprise occurs when the rise in the importance of information—and the need to secure it—is followed closely by these concerns: the attempts globally to steal intellectual property, to gain illegal access to information-as-product, and to enter value chains and achieve the ability to damage the information on which those chains rely.

A New Information Infrastructure

Changes in the IT infrastructures we must protect are far-reaching and include increased and ubiquitous use of mobile devices, advances in cloud technology (and changes in cloud business models), and the ongoing transition worldwide to Internet protocol version 6 (IPv6). We rely increasingly on mobile (physically untethered) devices for the bulk of our IT needs. These devices, smartphones and tablets, have become "convergence platforms" that serve all our digital needs, including telephony, e-mail, tweets and text messages, audio and video media, online commerce, financial transactions, and even supply chain management. Mobile devices are used to facilitate meetings and online conferences. They are sources of entertainment. They help us build and shape virtual communities worldwide. With the means to deploy more powerful applications, they support us in managing business.

Cost and efficiency drivers have made the transition to cloud architectures swifter than many foresaw. More and more enterprises are moving vital workloads to public clouds, private sectors, and "hybrid" cloud models. These workloads include enterprise resource management (ERM) and customer relations management (CRM) applications; development and test (devtest) environments, back-office, and enterprise applications; conferencing and multimedia applications; desktop applications; and supply chain management. Cloud cost models have become competitive and compelling. The ubiquity of cloud capacity has made cloud infrastructure "plastic," allowing enterprise to shift its workload from one cloud provider to another, depending on requirements, cost, and availability. This "cloud orchestration" model was pioneered by companies such as CSC through its acquisition of ServiceMesh. While offering an ever-more-efficient mechanism for managing availability and cost, the model complicates the association of data with any specific physical location, already a challenge in a world of complex cloud infrastructures hosted on myriad vast server farms. The recent European Commission decision to invalidate the 2000 Safe Harbor decision (allowing U.S.-based processing of European citizens' information) thrusts privacy concerns at the heart of the global cloud model.[9] The decision relates to the ongoing rise of privacy as an issue shaping cybersecurity discussed later.

Complicating this situation is the rise of IPv6 and the "Internet of Things" (IoT) that it makes possible. We are reaching the limits under the preceding Internet protocol version 4 (IPv4) of the number of devices (approximately four billion) that we can attach to the Internet with identifiable addresses. IPv6 will allow the connection and addressing of a number of devices[10] that can be described as greater than the number of stars in the known universe, squared![11] Other aspects of IPv6 make this protocol more efficient. Its adoption will create new and complex infrastructures that extend from our mobile devices through a "plastic" cloud to the very devices on which our lives depend. The adoption of IPv6 will allow for a more or less unfettered convergence of today's enterprise IT and the operational technology (OT) that controls physical infrastructures (e.g., energy, transportation, water, health care, etc.). Components of these infrastructures (turbines, valves, railway switches) are instrumented with IP-enabled devices that allow for the collection of data and more efficient and distributed command and control. Information can be used to mediate the resources associated with the emerging "smart grid," for example. For the electrical power sector, the Department of Energy describes such infrastructures as follows:

> "Smart grid" generally refers to a class of technology people are using to bring utility electricity delivery systems into the 21st century, using computer-based remote control and automation. These systems are made possible by two-way communication technology and computer processing that has been used for decades in other industries. They are beginning to be used on electricity networks, from the power plants and wind farms all the way to the consumers of electricity in homes and businesses. They offer many benefits to utilities and consumers—mostly seen in big improvements in energy efficiency on the electricity grid and in the energy users' homes and offices.[12]

It is likely that the emergence of IP-enabled, information-mediated infrastructures will allow for the "smart" management of combined systems, for example, electrical energy (for rechargeable, electric cars) and intelligence roadways serving self-driving cars. Such technology could allow drivers to make cost- and time-efficient decisions about when to recharge their cars and when to run routine errands, combining an understanding of electrical power costs with regional transportation congestion.

This article offers a framework for analysis regarding the evolving cybersecurity landscape. However, the author's business background makes irresistible a few words on the likely implications of these infrastructure changes on the nature of the cybersecurity business. The management of cybersecurity on an enterprise basis is something many enterprises undertake for themselves, either by constituting their own cybersecurity workforce or by using a cybersecurity services provider to manage the various cybersecurity tools and technologies (e.g., firewalls, governance/risk/compliance tools, intrusion detection/protection systems, antivirus tools, security information, and event management systems) in which the enterprise has invested. Some enterprises are outsourcing their cybersecurity, in whole or in part, to commercial managed security services providers (MSSPs), acquiring (cyber)security-as-a-service (or SaaS). The model of cybersecurity managed internally is likely to become more difficult to implement, particularly given the "plastic" nature of the infrastructures being safeguarded, the shift to multiple cloud backbones on which they will rely, the interconnected nature of these infrastructures (e.g., connected to suppliers, partners, and customers), and the extension of these networks to IPv6-enabled manufacturing and critical infrastructure appliances. Enterprises will be hard-pressed to maintain an accurate infrastructure topology, much less deploying to these infrastructures and managing the cybersecurity tools and technologies they elect to use. MSSPs specializing in cybersecurity are more likely to have the expertise requisite to meeting this challenge. They will be required to develop business models, metrics (and associated service-level agreements), and pricing models that reflect shifting and interconnected infrastructures. They will need both to manage cybersecurity devices in the enterprises for which they are taking responsibility *and* to understand and help protect other infrastructures on which their clients' infrastructures depend. In effect, as IT capacity becomes a managed commodity, so too might become the cybersecurity needed to safeguard that capacity.

The implications of this change in the infrastructure landscape are important to consider. More complex infrastructures will be more difficult to characterize. Anomalous behavior caused by cyber exploits and attacks may be more difficult to detect. Shared infrastructures complicate the challenge of monitoring and managing cybersecurity by any one enterprise or MSSP. Infrastructures that change quickly will need cybersecurity management tools and technologies that can characterize and assess and dynamically mitigate cybersecurity vulnerabilities, incidents, and consequences. Overall, our ability to understand complex, changing systems will require cybersecurity tools for monitoring, analysis, and response that exceed current cybersecurity technology.

The Threat Changes

Changes in the threat landscape have resulted in breaches that have become larger both in the number of people whose information has been compromised and the depth of that compromise (i.e., the range of attributes reflecting personal information, including social security numbers, financial information, security clearance information, and even biometric data such as fingerprints). Foreign intelligence organizations and cyber criminals have demonstrated impressive access to and use of sophisticated cyber exploit technologies. In the case of Stuxnet and possibly a German steel manufacturing plant, cyber-attack technologies can penetrate the industrial control systems (ICS) that connect physical systems with IT infrastructures.[13]

New malware can exhibit no known signature (before its first use). It is polymorphic (adept in changing its appearance once rooted in a target infrastructure), able to hide and evade the "sandboxing" used to isolate it within a target infrastructure, stealthy, and capable of "beaconing" to and responding effective command and control by its handlers. Stuxnet malware purportedly targeted Iranian centrifuges used to produce highly enriched uranium. It supposedly consisted of numerous "zero-day" modules (not seen before) and was capable of identifying specific components of the ICS used by Iranian centrifuges. It tricked those systems into spinning the centrifuges at incorrect rotations, while informing the workstations used to monitor them that the centrifuges' operation was normal. Such malware is indeed "advanced."

Perhaps more troubling is the advance in operational expertise or "tradecraft" exhibited by cyber exploiters and attackers. This tradecraft is characterized by formal information requirements, well-defined doctrine and operational concepts, thorough reconnaissance and intelligence characterization of the targeted infrastructure, dedicated resources capable of treating the infrastructures to be penetrated as formal intelligence targets, and impressive persistence—lasting almost ten years (and possibly more)—and the malware posed by organizations that possess this tradecraft can be characterized as "persistent." In other words, malware and the operations that employ it can be called "advanced persistent threats" or APTs. The use of operational expertise extends to clever social network analysis (to identify users with administrative privileges, for example) and well-targeted spear-phishing that can result in the compromise of privileged information by even well-trained IT professionals. The use of witting and unwitting insiders whose administrative privileges can be compromised can undermine network defenses significantly. Of equal importance, constant changes in the IT infrastructures we seek to defend leave defenders unable to accurately characterize their own networks. On the other hand, exploiters and attackers can operate with the discipline of well-established intelligence services. They can form a more accurate view of the networks they threaten than the view held by the networks' owners.

Reporting abounds that characterizes the manner in which cybersecurity threats have become technically advanced and operationally efficient. Employees of the author's company, ICF International, working with the Army's Research Laboratory's Threat Cell, see evidence of the increased technical sophistication of today's malware. Mandiant, a cybersecurity professional services subsidiary of FireEye, publishes an annual report that provides a year-over-year view of the technical and operational cybersecurity threat landscape.[14] Mandiant's report paints an alarming picture of the cybersecurity challenges facing modern, information-intensive enterprises, including the difficulty in finding malware before law enforcement or social media becomes aware of these enterprises' breaches. Mandiant noted,

> [In 2014] attackers still had a free rein in breached environments far too long before being detected—a median of 205 days in 2014 compared with 229 days in 2013. At the same time, the number of organizations discovering these intrusions on their own remained largely unchanged. Sixty-nine percent learned of the breach from an outside entity such as law enforcement. That's up from 67 percent in 2013 and 63 percent in 2012.[15]

Mandiant's report added that at least one breach had remained undetected for 2,982 days, a period consistent with the author's own experience dealing with a breach that had been undetected (and unmitigated) for approximately nine years. Speaking to the adaptability of today's cyber adversaries, Mandiant also noted,

> As security teams deploy new defenses, attackers are evolving their tactics. We saw that dynamic in full force over the past year as attackers employed new tactics (or in some cases sharpened tried-and-true techniques from the past) to hijack virtual private networking security, evade detection, steal credentials; and maintain a stealthy, persistent foothold in compromised environments.[16]

The report reflects eloquently both the technical prowess and operational cunning with which today's cybersecurity professionals must contend.[17]

Perhaps no cybersecurity incident illustrates the convergence of technology and tradecraft as the reported 2010–2011 compromise of the algorithm used in RSA's SecurID key fobs, employed by many organizations to govern access to sensitive IT systems. *Wired* magazine and others reported that the RSA breach was followed in swift order by compromises at a number of defense contractors (e.g., L-3 and Lockheed) that employ RSA's technology.[18] This set of incidents reflects a well-elaborated plan that defined the information the exploiter desired, determined where that information was managed and how it was protected, and compromised the technology used to protect that information. More important, this plan used that compromise swiftly—and before it could be detected and mitigated—to steal sensitive defense information. Such an operation reflects planning, discipline, readiness, and polished execution. The intellect and resources associated with such incidents represent a difficult challenge for any targeted enterprise.

The implications of the evolving threat landscape will force IT executives and operators to become more vigilant regarding the vulnerabilities of their enterprises. It will compel better threat information sharing and may prove an impetus to the formation of new information-sharing and advisory organizations, as described by a 2015 Presidential Executive Order.[19] Enterprises of all types will be forced to consider the strategies they need to defend themselves against threats posed in the past by nation-state actors against national security targets only. Even smaller enterprises may be subject to sophisticated cyber attacks and exploits by adversaries attempting to test their capabilities on such targets as a way of avoiding detection.

Cybersecurity in Peace, in War, and In-Between

Much has been written regarding the continuing efforts of the United States and others to achieve effective cyber defense in light of unending work by other countries and cyber criminals to exploit and damage sensitive information and achieve the ability to attack critical, IT-dependent infrastructures. In a previous article in the *Georgetown Journal on International Affairs*, the author contrasted the views of the United States and other Western democracies of cybersecurity as a discipline safeguarding intellectual property, infrastructures, and private information within a global commons (i.e., global cyberspace).[20] Russia and China, by contrast, view cybersecurity as the exercise of government authority within portions of cyberspace. These governments seek to exercise the prerogatives of sovereignty—principally to safeguard social stability and limit the effects of religious, political, and other movements these governments regard as illegitimate. Additional articles in the current volume of the *Georgetown Journal of International Affairs* and others describe the evolution of cybersecurity as an element of warfare and statecraft, evidence of the rising importance of cybersecurity (and cyberspace) as an element to which international relations theorists must pay attention. Indeed, rising importance to international relations and the functioning of the international system is one of the principal dynamics shaping the cybersecurity landscape.

The evolution of this dynamic, however, appears to be tending toward a situation in which cybersecurity challenges (exploits and attacks) are a constant concern. Rather than concerns about a "cyber war," we are witnessing cyber attacks and exploits as a component of statecraft in peacetime. They are tools "short of war" and components of hybrid warfare operations (e.g., Russia's campaign against Ukraine) that constitute neither peace nor war but allow countries to engage in conflict while maintaining diplomatic and economic relations. Efforts to steal and alter information, damage information infrastructures and IT-dependent critical infrastructures, and shape information conveyed through social and online media are ever present. Theorists such as Lucas Kello deride the term "cyber war" while seeking to describe this new state of affairs. These efforts also challenge international relations theorists generally to model cybersecurity challenges as factors modulating ongoing relations among countries and between countries and non-state actors. International relations practitioners now consider what behavioral norms are required to accommodate these challenges, while protecting the stability of the international system (and avoiding destabilizing surprises). Behavioral norms do not eliminate all behavior deemed objectionable by all actors, but they can constrain provocative behavior and non-proportional responses.

A survey of the field of the emerging role of cybersecurity as a component of the international system is not provided here. However, prominent international relations theorists are seeking to describe that role. Erik Gartzke's 2013 article, "The Myth of Cyberwar,"[21] notes that cyberwar is "unlikely to prove particularly potent in grand strategic terms."[22] Gartzke challenges various cyber-war concepts and notes,

- Cyber damage can be more easily repaired than damage to physical infrastructures.
- Countries that are the victims of covert cyber attack cannot acquiesce to attackers they do not know.
- Some cyber-attack capabilities risk being made ineffective after their first use.

Gartzke's article provides evidence that cyber attack as a challenge to cybersecurity is assuming its logical place alongside other tools in the exercise of power and influence, rather than as a decisive mode of combat.

The 2013 article by Lucas Kello, "The Meaning of the Cyber Revolution," offers a challenge to study the effects on the international system of cyber attacks and exploits.[23] Kello regards the term "cyber war" as overused.[24] He suggests assets used in the research methodologies to analyze international relations can and should be applied to the study of cybersecurity challenges. Kello quotes former National Security Agency (NSA) director and commander of the U.S. Cyber Command, General Keith Alexander, who stated that "no consensus exists" regarding how to characterize the destabilizing effects of cyber attack. Kello's work represents, as does Gartzke's, a challenge to theorists to replace speculation with useful research.

What might this research show? Recent events support the hypothesis that efforts are under way to establish norms as well as the diplomatic and political mechanisms required to react to normative transgressions. Although more research is necessary to convert this hypothesis to theory, recent events are noteworthy, perhaps none more so that the recent cybersecurity agreement between President Obama and Chinese president Xi Jinping.[25] An attempt at normative behavior can be seen in the following:

> The United States and China agree that neither country's government will conduct or knowingly support cyber-enabled theft of intellectual property, including trade secrets or other confidential business information, with the intent of providing competitive advantages to companies or commercial sectors.[26]

Although the agreement attempts to constrain the theft of intellectual property, it does not define the sanctions that might follow such theft. It is silent regarding cyber exploits by one government against the other, reflecting perhaps acceptance of such acts. Indeed, former Central Intelligence Agency and NSA director Michael Hayden has called the recent breach (possibly by China) of personal records held by the U.S. Office of Personnel Management as "honorable espionage work" against a "legitimate intelligence target."[27] In other words, the state of affairs in which the agreement was drafted reflects efforts to define normative behavior, although recognizing that some acts, while unpalatable, are not necessarily unacceptable. This agreement also represents, perhaps, an effort by the United States and China to interact in cyberspace without dangerous conflict, even in the presence of very different concepts of cybersecurity ("global commons" rather than "sovereign cyberspace"[28]).

For theorists of international relations, governments, non-state actors, warriors, and even the private sector, the implications of efforts to achieve and describe normative behavior are likely to be significant. The existence of norms recognizes that the behavior associated with those norms will be present under day-to-day circumstances. Government departments and agencies—and their industrial partners—will need to detect, fend off, and mitigate foreign cyber exploits that do not reflect the theft of intellectual property intended to create commercial advantage. Defense contractors, for example, may find that exploits against their systems, while unfortunate, do not violate necessarily emerging norms, thus making more likely such exploits and more important the need to deal with them. If this trend holds, we are likely to see a continuing shift from concerns about "cyber war" to recognition that some level of cyber exploit is part of the "new normal."

The same may be true regarding cyber attack. Sascha Dov Bachmann and Håkan Gunneriusson argue in a 2015 article that Russia has built a hybrid warfare doctrine that incorporates attacks against another country's infrastructure into an operational approach that falls just short of war.[29] Russia is using this doctrine in Ukraine. The country is combining cyber attacks, efforts to shape online and social media discussions, support to Ukrainian separatists, deployment of Russian irregulars, and the unacknowledged use of Russian soldiers into an effective campaign, one that is eroding the Ukrainian government's effectiveness while corroding the integrity of Ukraine's border with Russia. Again, the implications are likely to be significant. Russia's doctrine represents the use of force "short of war" and drives those affected (government, non-government, and commercial entities and others) to exist in a state in which attacks against their IT infrastructures are unpalatable but not regarded as acts of war and not compelling a vigorous, warlike response.

Overall, the international system will need to adjust to accommodate cybersecurity challenges as a factor that is both constantly present and constantly changing. Low barriers to entry, difficulties with attribution (of exploits and attacks), and modest consequences (to date) faced by the perpetrators of cyber attacks and exploits are likely to make these activities a long-term aspect of the international system.

Privacy Dominates—for Now

The 2006 CNCI defines cybersecurity as a national security imperative, one that unites the public and private sectors. From a policy perspective, CNCI makes clear that an enduring public interest exists in the cybersecurity of the defense industrial base, critical infrastructure, and parts of the nation's manufacturing base as well as the national defense, intelligence, and civil government establishment.

Things have changed.

Today's cybersecurity environment is defined increasingly by concerns about privacy and a perceived need to protect private information from government authorities. Examples abound, and one can speculate as to the reasons for this shift, though Edward Snowden's activities appear to be the most influential.

Three examples cast into sharp relief this change in the cybersecurity narrative. First, the 2000 Safe Harbor decision by the European Commission indicated that U.S. data protection standards are adequate for European Union citizens.[30] The intervening years, however, have wrought visible change in the European political situation vis-à-vis U.S. data privacy, as reflected in an October 2015 decision by the Commission that U.S. data protection standards are not sufficient. Taking place against the backdrop of enduring European concerns over the purported activities of the U.S. intelligence community and a case brought in 2013 by an Austrian citizen, the court's ruling invalidated the 2000 U.S.-EU Safe Harbor Agreement. It also determined that member countries' data protection authorities are not bound by the commission, allowing for further challenges. Although the U.S. government is working vigorously to restore Safe Harbor, this ruling reflects a trans-Atlantic cybersecurity relationship defined as much by privacy concerns as by the needs for mutual defense.

Second, broad agreement appears to exist on the need to improve public and private cybersecurity threat and incident information sharing. However, successive bills brought forward in the U.S. House and Senate (the Cybersecurity Information Sharing and Protection Act [CISPA] and the Cybersecurity Information Sharing Act [CISA], respectively), have foundered on the rocks of concerns raised by privacy and civil liberties advocates. The bills did not advance to the president's desk from 2010 to 2014. Indeed, rumors abounded in Washington that the president would veto an information-sharing bill that risked the unauthorized (even mistaken) disclosure of private information to the government generally and the intelligence community specifically. In addition, members of the IT industry feared the potential liability that could result should such a disclosure take place, reflecting their customers' private information. Only in October 2015 was a Senate bill presented that appeared capable of gaining White House support. The Senate bill is prescriptive in its protections of information considered private.[31] Conditional administration support was signaled in a statement of administration policy, although that statement emphasizes that information sharing must be mediated through the Department of Homeland Security.[32] Although not entirely satisfactory to the civil liberties community, the bill passed both houses and gained presidential signature.

Finally, one notes that conservative congressional leaders, including two reported candidates for the position of Speaker of the House of Representatives—a position to which Congressman Paul Ryan (R-Wisconsin) has been elected—are known more for their concerns regarding cybersecurity privacy than for cybersecurity as a national security issue. Congressman Darrell Issa (R-California) has made clear his view that NSA's bulk collection programs (specifically, the program authorized by Section 215 of the Patriot Act) should be limited.[33] Congressman Jason Chaffetz (R-Utah) and Issa both support the Email Privacy Act, which would close a loophole in the Electronic Communication Privacy Act that "allows the government to subpoena e-mails from Internet service providers after they're 180-days old."[34]

Taken together, these examples point to a cybersecurity landscape domestically that is influenced more powerfully by privacy concerns than in the past. They represent a likely reaction to the purported actions of the government in cyberspace as well as a change internationally. They also reflect a clear division between the United States and many of its partners. This division, defined by privacy concerns, stands in contrast to the continuing but now less prominent efforts to work together in support of common cyber defense. Whether privacy will trump national security in defining the cybersecurity relationship between the United States and its European allies (and other countries) remains to be seen. National security may reassert itself (particularly in the wake of the November 2015 terrorist attacks in Paris), or a new accommodation between national security and privacy may be struck. In any case, the cybersecurity landscape with which policymakers and operators will be forced to deal will be shaped by these parallel, often entwined considerations as will the relations among allies and between allies and other countries.

Some Progress Is Evident

While this article proposes an analytical framework, it is worth noting that progress has been made, particularly on the part of the U.S. government. This progress, which is itself a framework, consists of

- a presidential policy directive (21) that identifies sixteen critical infrastructure standards that require stronger cybersecurity;[35]
- a presidential executive order (EO 13636) mandating the creation by the National Institute of Standards and Technology (NIST) a cybersecurity framework that identifies best practices, provides a means for critical infrastructure self-assessment, and conveys a mechanisms for sector-specific cybersecurity standards; and[36]
- an additional executive order that mandates the creation of information sharing and advisory organizations (ISAOs) to improve cybersecurity threat and best-practice information sharing within specific sectors and for specialized needs (e.g., the operational technology used in industrial control systems).[37]

Another framework we should mention is the Tallinn Manual, a NATO-sponsored effort that seeks to codify the rules of conduct of offensive cyber operations.[38] The manual represents an effort to impose on nation-states a set of behavior norms, improving transparency and predictability and possibly improve our understanding of the role of cybersecurity in the international system.

While useful, this progress should be accompanied by a stronger understanding of the larger context of information value, global policy, and operations shaping cyberspace today and tomorrow and the cybersecurity challenge we face.

Conclusion

The cybersecurity field is changing swiftly. The swiftness of this change makes difficult the detachment generally useful to gain perspective and balance, to generate hypotheses, and to collect the data necessary to theorize. At the same time, the swiftness of these changes poses challenges to policymakers, operators, technologists, and practitioners. This article identifies major categories of change and provides the means to describe the evolving cybersecurity landscape in a manner that is both lucid and practical. Governments and commercial enterprises must shape policies that reflect the concerns of citizens and customers alike. Governments and commercial enterprises must recognize the ever-present threats that are likely to endure and grow more serious in a world where cyber exploits and cyber attacks can take place at any time and may become regarded as "peacetime," normative behavior. Defending against these attacks and exploits will be made more difficult by the rising value of the information at risk and the complexity of the infrastructures by which this information is managed and which this information helps control. The framework provided, framed by salient issues, represents a useful starting point for the further analysis of cyber developments—and possibly a challenge to develop stronger and more useful frameworks in future.

Notes

1. "The Comprehensive National Cybersecurity Initiative," White House, undated, https://www.whitehouse.gov/issues/foreign-policy/cybersecurity/national-initiative.
2. "Cybersecurity—Executive Order 13636," White House, February 12, 2013 https://www.whitehouse.gov/the-press-office/2013/02/12/executive-order-improving-critical-infrastructure-cybersecurity.
3. Department of Information Technology & Operations Management, Florida Atlantic University, and Jim Quan, Department of Information Technology & Operations Management, Florida Atlantic University.
4. Kevin Gosling, "E-Enabled Capabilities of the 787 Dreamliner," *Aero Quarterly*, Qtr. 01.09, http://www.boeing.com/commercial/aeromagazine/articles/qtr_01_09/article_05_1.html.
5. Ibid.
6. "How Information Gives You Competitive Advantage," *Harvard Business Review* 63, no. 2 (1985).
7. Ibid.
8. Sunil Mithas and Jonathan Whitaker, "Is the World Flat or Spiky? Information Intensity, Skills, and Global Service Disaggregation," *Information Systems Research* 18 no. 3 (2007): 237–59, http://terpconnect.umd.edu/~smithas/papers/mithaswhitaker2007isr.pdf.
9. "How Many Addresses Can Ipv6 Hold?" *itsnobody* (blog), February 17, 2012, https://itsnobody.wordpress.com/2012/02/17/how-many-addresses-can-ipv6-hold/.
10. 2128, or 340,282,366,920,938,463,463,374, 607,431,768,211,456.
11. Difference Between.net, "Difference Between IPv4 and IPv6," available at http://www.differencebetween.net/technology/internet/difference-between-ipv4-and-ipv6/.
12. "Smart Grid," Office of Electricity Delivery and Energy Reliability, U.S. Department of Energy, undated, http://energy.gov/oe/services/technology-development/smart-grid.
13. See http://www.icfi.com/insights/white-papers/2015/germany-cyber-weapons-test
14. *M-Trends® 2015: A View from the Front Lines*, Mandiant, https://www2.fireeye.com/WEB-2015-MNDT-RPT-M-Trends-2015_LP.html.
15. Ibid.
16. Ibid.
17. At the same time, it is important to acknowledge that much reporting and accompanying analysis has yet to benefit from consistent methodology. Too much information remains anecdotal. Beyond the scope of this article, but clearly vital, is the need to improve quantitative cybersecurity research.
18. Kevin Poulsen, "Second Defense Contractor L-3 'Actively Targeted' with RSA Secured Hacks," *Wired*, May 31, 2011, http://www.wired.com/2011/05/l-3/.
19. Executive Order—Promoting Private Sector Cybersecurity Information Sharing, White House, February 13, 2015, https://www.whitehouse.gov/the-press-office/2015/02/13/executive-order-promoting-private-sector-cybersecurity-information-shari.
20. Samuel S. Visner, "Cybersecurity's Next Agenda," *Georgetown Journal of International Affairs* (2014): 93–103.

21. Erik Gartzke, "The Myth of Cyberwar: Bringing War in Cyberspace Back Down to Earth," *International Security* 38, no. 2 (Fall 2013): 41–73, doi:10.1162/ISEC_a_00136.
22. Gartzke writes, "Key limitations exist regarding what can be achieved over the internet. It is one thing for an opponent to interrupt a country's infrastructure, communications, or military coordination and planning. It is another to ensure that the damage inflicted translates into a lasting shift in the balance of national power or resolve. Cyber attacks are unlikely to prove particularly potent in grand strategic terms unless they can impose substantial, durable harm on an adversary. In many, perhaps most, circumstances, this will occur only if cyberwar is accompanied by terrestrial military force or other actions designed to capitalize on any temporary incapacity achieved via the internet. Those initiating cyber attacks must therefore decide whether they are prepared to exploit the windows of opportunity generated by internet attacks through other modes of combat. If they are not willing and able to do so, then in grand strategic terms, there are few compelling reasons to initiate cyberwar. The need to back up cyber with other modes of conflict in turn suggests that the chief beneficiaries of cyberwar are less likely to be marginal groups or rising challengers looking to overturn the existing international order and more likely to be nation-states that already possess important terrestrial military advantages. Conceived of in this way, the internet poses no revolution in military affairs but instead promises simply to extend existing international disparities in power and influence." Ibid., 43.
23. Lucas Kello, "The Meaning of the Cyber Revolution," *International Security* 38, no. 2 (Fall 2013): 7–40, doi:10.1162/ISEC_a_00138.
24. Kello interview, "Episode 21: Lucas Kello and International Security editor Sean Lynn-Jones on Cyber Security," available at MIT Press Journals Podcast Series, http://www.mitpressjournals.org/page/podcast_episode21_ISEC.
25. "Fact Sheet: President Xi Jinping's State Visit to the United States," White House, September 25, 1015, https://www.whitehouse.gov/the-press-office/2015/09/25/fact-sheet-president-xi-jinpings-state-visit-united-states.
26. Ibid.
27. "The Best Offense: Former CIA Head: OPM Hack was 'Honorable Espionage Work,'" *American Interest*, June 16, 2015, http://www.the-american-interest.com/2015/06/16/former-cia-head-opm-hack-was-honorable-espionage-work/.
28. Visner, "Cybersecurity's Next Agenda."
29. Sascha Dov Bachmann and Håkan Gunneriusson, "Russia's Hybrid Warfare in the East: The Integral Nature of the Information Sphere," *Georgetown Journal of International Affairs*, Cyber V issue, October 2, 2015.
30. Ellen Nakashima, "National Security: Top E.U. Court Strikes Down Major Data-Sharing Pact Between U.S. and Europe," *Washington Post*, October 6, 2015, https://www.washingtonpost.com/world/national-security/eu-court-strikes-down-safe-harbor-data-transfer-deal-over-privacy-concerns/2015/10/06/2da2d9f6-6c2a-11e5-b31c-d80d62b53e28_story.html.
31. Section 105(a)(1) notes that cybersecurity systems must: "(A) limit the effect on privacy and civil liberties of activities by the Federal Government 19 under this title; (B) limit the receipt, retention, use, and dissemination of cyber threat indicators containing personal information or information that identifies specific persons, including by establishing—(i) a process for the timely destruction of such information that is known not to be directly related to uses authorized under this title; and (ii) specific limitations on the length of any period in which a cyber threat indicator may be retained; (C) include requirements to safeguard cyber threat indicators containing personal information or information that identifies specific persons from unauthorized access or acquisition, including appropriate sanctions for activities by officers, employees, or agents of the Federal Government in contravention of such guidelines; (D) include procedures for notifying entities and Federal entities if information received pursuant to this section is known or determined by a Fed-

eral entity receiving such information not to constitute a cyber threat indicator; (E) protect the confidentiality of cyber threat indicators containing personal information or information that identifies specific persons to the greatest extent practicable and require recipients to be informed that such indicators may only be used for purposes authorized under this title; and (F) include steps that may be needed so that dissemination of cyber threat indicators is consistent with the protection of classified and other sensitive national security information."

32. Executive Office of the President, Office of Management and Budget, "Statement of Administration Policy, S. 754—Cybersecurity Information Sharing Act of 2015," October 22, 2015, https://www.whitehouse.gov/sites/default/files/omb/legislative/sap/114/saps754s_20151022.pdf.
33. Guiseppe Macri, "Issa: Government Can Help the Internet of Things by Staying out of It," *InsideSources*, May 21, 2015, http://www.insidesources.com/issa-government-can-help-the-internet-of-things-by-staying-out-of-it/.
34. Guiseppe Macri, "Could Silicon Valley Get a Speaker of the House?" *InsideSources*, October 14, 2015, http://www.insidesources.com/could-silicon-valley-get-a-speaker-of-the-house/.
35. "Executive Order (EO) 13636 Improving Critical Infrastructure Cybersecurity Presidential Policy Directive (PPD)-21 Critical Infrastructure Security and Resilience," Homeland Security, March 2013, https://www.dhs.gov/sites/default/files/publications/EO-13636-PPD-21-Fact-Sheet-508.pdf.
36. "Improving Critical Infrastructure Cybersecurity, Executive Order 13636: Preliminary Cybersecurity Framework," http://www.nist.gov/itl/upload/preliminary-cybersecurity-framework.pdf.
37. Executive Order—Promoting Private Sector Cybersecurity Information Sharing, White House, February 13, 2015.
38. Tallinn Manual Process, CCDCOE, https://ccdcoe.org/tallinn-manual.html.

Military Matters

Constraining Norms for Cyber Warfare Are Unlikely

Brian M. Mazanec

The question of whether constraining international norms for cyber warfare will emerge and thrive is of paramount importance to the unfolding age of cyber conflict. This is a pivotal question, as highlighted by recent testimony from Director of National Intelligence Jim Clapper when he stated, "The growing use of cyber capabilities . . . is also outpacing the development of a shared understanding of norms of behavior, increasing the chances for miscalculations and misunderstandings that could lead to unintended escalation."[1] Some scholars think that great powers will inevitably cooperate and establish rules, norms, and standards for cyberspace.[2] While it is true that increased competition may create incentives for cooperation on constraining norms, norm evolution theory for emerging-technology weapons leads one to conclude that constraining norms for cyber warfare will face many challenges and may never successfully emerge.

Some of these challenges were also presented by the advent of the other emerging-technology weapons in historic cases, such as chemical and biological weapons, strategic bombing, and nuclear weapons. An analysis of these three historic examples offers valuable lessons that lead to the development of norm evolution theory tailored for emerging-technology weapons, which can then be applied to cyber warfare to better evaluate whether or not the authors' conclusions are well founded. This article does exactly that, first by defining emerging-technology weapons and norm evolution theory and then briefly reviewing the current state of international norms for cyber warfare. Next, it illustrates norm evolution theory for emerging-technology weapons—grounded in the three historic case studies—and prospects for current norms among China, Russia, and the United States. Third, it presents a refined theory of norm development as a framework to evaluate norm emergence that contradicts the authors' thesis. This argument leads to the conclusion that a constraining international order in cyberspace is far from inevitable.

Emerging-Technology Weapons and Norm Evolution Theory

Emerging-technology weapons are weapons based on new technology or a novel employment of older technologies to achieve certain effects. Given that technology is constantly advancing, weapons that initially fall into this category will eventually no longer be considered emergent. For ex-

Brian M. Mazanec is an assistant director for defense capabilities and management with the U.S. government and an adjunct professor in the School of Policy, Government, and International Affairs, the Department of Public and International Affairs, at George Mason University. He has written on cyber and national security issues and is the author of the book *The Evolution of Cyber War: International Norms for Emerging Technology Weapons* and coauthor of the book *Deterring Cyber Warfare: Bolstering Strategic Stability in Cyberspace.*

ample, the gunpowder-based weapons that began to spread in fourteenth-century Europe would clearly be classified as emerging-technology weapons in that century and perhaps in the fifteenth century but eventually these weapons were no longer novel and became fairly ubiquitous.[3] Chemical weapons up to the early twentieth century could be considered an emerging-technology weapon. Likewise, strategic bombing up to World War II also falls into this category. Nuclear and biological weapons could be considered emerging-technology weapons during World War II and the immediate years that followed. Today cyber weapons used to conduct computer network attack (CNA) are emerging-technology weapons. In general, norm evolution theory identifies three major stages in a norm's potential life cycle. These three stages are (1) norm emergence, (2) norm cascade, and (3) norm internalization.[4] The primary hypothesis of norm evolution theory for emerging-technology weapons is that a state's self-interest will play a significant role; a norm's convergence with perceived state self-interest will be important to achieving norm emergence and a state acting as a norm leader. It further states that norms are more likely to emerge when vital actors are involved, specifically key states acting as norm leaders and norm entrepreneurs within organizations. The two primary intergovernmental bodies and organizations currently being used to promote emerging norms for cyber warfare are the United Nations (UN) and the North Atlantic Treaty Organization (NATO). Additionally, there are some other key multilateral efforts to encourage the development of cyber norms, such as the London Conference on Cyberspace and academic cyber norm workshops.

The Case for Norm Evolution Theory

What does norm evolution theory for emerging-technology weapons predict regarding the development of constrictive international norms? The three examples of chemical and biological weapons, strategic bombing, and nuclear weapons are particularly salient historic case studies when considering norm evolution for cyber warfare for a variety of reasons.

Chemical and biological weapons and cyber weapons are both nonconventional weapons that share many of the same special characteristics with significant international security implications.[5] Owing to these characteristics, both of these weapons are also attractive to non-state actors or those seeking anonymity resulting in a lack of clarity regarding the responsible party.

Strategic bombing—particularly with the advent of airpower as an emerging-technology weapon and the early use of airplanes to drop bombs on cities—forced states to grapple with a brand new technology and approach to warfare, as is now the case with cyber warfare. As with chemical and biological weapons, strategic bombing shares some special characteristics with cyber warfare. Strategic bombing made civilian populations highly vulnerable, was difficult to defend against, and used technology which also had peaceful applications such as air travel and transport—all of which can also be said about cyber warfare today. The effort to constrain strategic bombing through normative influences was mixed and at times completely unsuccessful, which makes it particularly well suited as an exemplar of the limits of norms and the way other factors may impede or reverse norm development.

Finally, nuclear weapons, like airpower before it and perhaps cyber weapons today, presented states with a challenge of a completely new and emerging war-fighting technology. Nuclear weapons and cyber weapons, like the other emerging-technology case studies, share many of the same special characteristics with significant international security implications. These include the potential for major collateral damage or unintended consequences (due to fallout, in the case of nuclear weapons) and covert development programs. Because of these common attributes, lessons regarding norm development can be learned and a framework developed that is applicable to predicting the prospects of constraining norms as a tool to address the use of cyber weapons.

Examining how norm evolution theory, informed by the three historic case studies, specifically applies to norms for emerging-technology weapons allows for a more informed prediction regarding the prospects of norm emergence for cyber warfare.[6] When these three case studies are considered, the primary reason for developing constraining norms for emerging-technology weapons is the perception among powerful or relevant states that such norms are in their national self-interest. That is, a direct or indirect alignment of national self-interest with a constraining norm leads to norm emergence and the extent to which it is aligned with key or powerful states' perception of self-interest will determine how rapidly and effectively the norm emerges. The role of national self-interest as the primary ingredient leading to norm emergence also helps explain why, when challenged with violations of a young and not-yet-internalized norm, a state is quick to abandon the norm and pursue its material interest by using the previously constrained emerging-technology weapon, as was seen with both chemical and biological weapons and strategic bombing in World War I and World War II.

Prospects for Cyber Warfare Norms

The key principle of norm evolution theory for emerging-technology weapons is that norm emergence is more likely to occur when powerful, relevant actors are involved, specifically key states acting as norm leaders and norm entrepreneurs within organizations. There are a variety of intergovernmental bodies and organizations currently being used by a variety of states to promote various emerging norms for cyber warfare. Through these organizations, a variety of actors, motivated by a number of factors and employing a range of mechanisms, have promoted various candidate cyber norms. These norms range from a total prohibition on cyber weapons and warfare to a no first-use policy or the applicability of the existing laws of armed conflict to cyber warfare. Norm evolution theory would thus seem to interpret this as a sign of progress for norm emergence. However, if one examines these efforts more closely, the prospects are less hopeful.

Powerful States, Constraining Norms, and Self-Interest

Powerful self-interested state actors will play a significant role in norm emergence. Additionally, perceived state self-interest will be important for norms to emerge and for a state to become a leader of a particular norm. Successful norm emergence requires states to act as norm leaders and increasing multipolarity is unlikely to help. After all, there were eight great powers in 1910, and that complicated rather than fueled the convergence of a constraining norm for strategic bombing. Since there is generally less exposure and understanding surrounding cyber weapons as well as different rates of weapon adoption and cyber vulnerability, states will be reluctant to lead on the issue of norms because they may be unable to determine the utility of such weapons relative to their own interests. However, such calculations are essential if important and powerful states are going to become strong norm leaders and help promote the emerging norm. Additionally, specific to China, Russia, and the United States—the preeminent cyber actors—an analysis of their respective cyber doctrines indicates the perspective that each nation has more to gain from engaging in cyber warfare than from significantly restricting it or giving it up entirely. National investments in cyber warfare capabilities and the development of doctrine and strategies for cyber warfare provide insight into state perceptions of self-interest and the expectations for behavior and emerging norms for cyber warfare. So where do state cyber warfare programs stand today in China, Russia, and the United States? The three key states discussed here are the most significant, both because of the breadth and sophistication of their capabilities and activities and because of the likelihood that they are serving as the model for many other nations preparing to operate in cyberspace.

Chinese Interest in Cyber Warfare

China's early activity and interest in cyber warfare indicate that it likely does not consider the emergence of constraining norms in its self-interest. It has been largely unconstrained by cyber norms and is preparing to use cyber weapons to cause economic harm, damage critical infrastructure, and influence kinetic armed conflict. As such, it is unlikely to be a vocal norm leader. China is best known for its expansive efforts conducting espionage-style cyber operations. For example, in February 2013, the U.S. cybersecurity firm Mandiant released a study detailing extensive and systematic cyber attacks, originating from Chinese military facilities of at least 141 separate U.S.-affiliated commercial and government targets and in May 2014 the Department of Justice indicted five Chinese military hackers for computer network exploitation (CNE) activity in the United States.[7] These attacks have led the U.S. Department of Defense to classify China as "the world's most active and persistent perpetrator of economic espionage" and point out that the country is also "looking at ways to use cyber for offensive operations."[8] It is this latter point that is of most interest to this article. China is increasingly developing and fielding advanced capabilities in cyberspace while its interests in cyber warfare appear to be asymmetric and strategic. China and the United States agreed in September 2015 that they will not knowingly conduct CNE theft of intellectual property for commercial advantage; however, there is evidence China is not living up to its end of the bargain.[9]

Russian Interest in Cyber Warfare

Like China's, Russia's early cyber warfare activity—especially the attacks on Estonia, Georgia, and Ukraine—indicates that it is largely unconstrained by restrictive cyber norms and is preparing to use cyber weapons in a wide range of conflicts and against a variety of targets. It likely does not consider the emergence of constraining norms in its self-interest. Thus, one would think it unlikely to be a vocal norm leader. However, Russia has been a leading proponent of a total ban on cyber weapons. This is similar to the Soviet Union's efforts early in the nuclear era to demonize U.S. possession of nuclear weapons while simultaneously pursuing such weapons themselves. It helps illustrate how powerful states acting in their own self-interest can inadvertently act as norm leaders despite flouting the candidate norm itself. However, Russia's confusing support for fully constraining norms for cyber warfare (its behavior in the UN and proposal for an "International Code of Conduct for

Information Security") may be based on its broader definition of cyber warfare and its interest in using a constraining norm to prevent what it perceives as "propaganda" inside Russia and in its near abroad.[10] But its position may also be disingenuous, as it was when supporting the Biological Weapons Convention while simultaneously launching a massive, illicit biological weapons program. To achieve any real convergence among the main cyber actors the authoritarian interest in constraining free speech must be addressed, which could deflate Russian support. Further, Russian doctrine now states that future conflict will entail the early implementation of cyber attack.[11]

U.S. Interest in Cyber Warfare

While China is perhaps the noisiest and Russia the most secretive when it comes to cyber warfare, the United States is the most sophisticated. The United States is in the process of dramatically expanding its military organization committed to engaging in cyber warfare and regularly engages in "offensive cyber operations."[12] However, unlike Russia and China, the United States appears to exercise restraint and avoid targeting nonmilitary targets. This seems to indicate that the United States is acting as a norm leader for at least a certain category of constraining cyber norms, although its general "militarization" of cyberspace may be negating the norm-promoting effects of this restraint. While the United States has recently developed classified rules of engagement for cyber warfare, it has articulated few, if any, limits on its use of force in cyberspace or response to hostile cyber attacks. For example, the May 2011 *International Strategy for Cyberspace* states that the United States "reserves the right to use all necessary means" to defend itself and its allies and partners, but that it will "exhaust all options before [the use of] military force."[13] Additionally, the former U.S. deputy secretary of defense, William Lynn, clearly asserted that "the United States reserves the right, under the law of armed conflict, to respond to serious cyber attacks with an appropriate, proportional, and justified military response."[14] Ultimately, the United States' behavior and interest in cyber warfare indicate that it does not consider the emergence of robust constraining norms in its self-interest.

Secondary Factors Affecting Norm Emergence

Norm evolution theory for emerging-technology weapons also recognizes secondary reasons for development, which are examined here in more detail.[15]

Coherence with Existing Dominant Norms Is Unlikely

Should current trends continue, the outlook for coherence with exiting norms is not favorable when applied to cyber warfare. First, cyber norms will have difficulty achieving coherence with and grafting onto existing norms. Unfortunately, the success of a norm candidate for emerging-technology weapons also will depend in large part on the ability to achieve coherence by connecting the new weapon type to an existing category and thus beginning the process of grafting the new norm onto existing norms. While cyber weapons and cyber warfare have some commonalities with certain weapons, particularly unconventional and emerging-technology weapons, overall they are truly unique. In fact, they are so unique as to operate in their own new, man-made domain outside the normal domains of land, sea, air, and space. Thus, cyber norms lack obvious coherence with many prominent norms, and it is difficult for norm entrepreneurs to graft the candidate norms to existing norms. Perhaps the best option for success is the humanitarian norm underlying the existing laws of armed conflict, particularly the norm regarding the protection of civilians and minimization of collateral damage.[16] This is precisely what NATO's *Tallinn Manual on the International Law Applicable to Cyber Warfare* attempts to achieve by arguing that the laws of armed conflict apply to cyber warfare.[17] However, the lack of agreement on key terms and confusion over the spectrum of hostile cyber operations make coherence and grafting complex and difficult.[18]

It Is Too Late to Preemptively Establish Norms for Cyber Warfare

Another challenge for norm emergence is that it will be more successful if the candidate norm can be permanently and preemptively established before such weapons exist or are fully capable and widespread. With cyber warfare, the train has already left the station so to speak. James Lewis and the Center for Strategic and International Studies identified sixteen significant CNA-style cyber attacks between 2006 and 2013.[19] These included major attacks across the globe from the former Soviet states of Estonia and Georgia to Iran and Saudi Arabia. The opportunity for permanent preemptive establishment of a norm has long since passed.

Differing Perspectives on Future Capability and Threat Inflation

There will be challenges arising from both differing perspectives as to future capability as well as the prospect for threat inflation. While it is true cyber warfare has been demonstrated to some degree (e.g., Stuxnet), the hidden and secretive nature of cyberspace makes the actors and their intent unclear and thus limits the true demonstrative value of recent cyber attacks. This has the effect of creating competing theories and arguments as to future effectiveness and strategic impact. As a case in point, some (including former U.S. secretary of defense Leon Panetta) argue that cyber warfare poses a major threat and warn of a "cyber Pearl Harbor" or "cyber 9/11" moment when critical infrastructure is attacked. Others have argued that statements such as Panetta's are pure hyperbole and that cyber warfare poses no such dire threat and in fact may not even constitute warfare as properly defined.[20] In the December 2013 edition of *Foreign Affairs*, Thomas Rid argued not only that cyber attack is not a major threat, but that it will in fact "diminish rather than accentuate political violence" by offering states and other actors a new mechanism to engage in aggression below the threshold of war.[21] Erik Gartzke argued further that cyber warfare is "unlikely to prove as pivotal in world affairs . . . as many observers seem to believe."[22] However, cybersecurity is a huge and booming business for information-technology security firms, with industry market research firms predicting the global cybersecurity market will grow from $106.32 billion in 2015 to $170.21 billion by 2020.[23] IT-security expert Bruce Schneier has alleged that these firms benefitting from cyber growth have, along with their government customers, artificially hyped the cyber threat.[24] Some critics have gone so far as to refer to this dynamic as "cyber doom" rhetoric or a "cybersecurity-industrial complex" similar to the oft-derided "defense-industrial complex."[25] Norm evolution theory applied in this case indicates that these vastly different perceptions as to the impact and role of cyber warfare in international relations and conflict will impair norm emergence, as was the case early in the twentieth century when the role and impact of strategic airpower was highly contested.

Defenseless Perception Impact

The idea that cyber weapons cannot be defended against will fuel interest in a constraining norm but also limit the effectiveness of reciprocal agreements and possibly lead to weapon proliferation. As a result, once convention-dependent norms are violated, intense domestic pressure can build for retaliatory violations of the norm. Defenses against cyber weapons are largely viewed as inadequate, and therefore, a sense of defenselessness persists. A report from the DoD's Defense Science Board reported in January 2013 that the United States "cannot be confident" critical IT systems can be defended from a well-resourced cyber adversary.[26] The nature of cyberspace, with intense secrecy and "zero-day" vulnerabilities, makes defense particularly difficult and fuels interest in other strategies to manage the threat, including constraining international norms. This explains the broad range of actors and organizations involved in early norm promotion and is a positive factor for the successful emergence of norms for cyber warfare. However, the experience of norms for emerging-technology weapons with similar perceptions regarding the weakness of defenses also indicates that while this may fuel interest in cultivating norms, they will be fragile and largely apply to use and not proliferation. This is because actors will continue to develop and pursue the weapons as they believe they cannot rely on defenses and seek deterrence-in-kind capabilities. Further, if the early norm is violated, given the inability to defend against continued violations, there may be domestic pressure to respond in kind, leading to a rapid erosion of the norm. Should early cyber norms be violated, such domestic pressure for an in-kind response could build. In fact, the Iranian attack on Saudi Aramco in August 2012 is largely viewed as one of Iran's responses to Stuxnet.[27] The challenge of attribution in cyberspace may accentuate this dynamic by making retaliatory responses even easier than with prior emerging-technology weapons.

Unitary Dominance and Delayed Proliferation and Adoption

Finally, weapon proliferation and adoption will play a significant role in norm emergence as it will influence state interest in constraining norms. For cyber warfare, there is not the kind of unitary dominance of a single actor as there was with the U.S. nuclear monopoly early in the age of nuclear—giving the United States significant influence on norm emergence regarding nuclear restraint. Additionally, given the ongoing proliferation of cyber weapons, the multiuse nature of the technology, and the relatively low cost of entry, delays in proliferating cyber weapons is unlikely. However, there will likely be varied rates of adoption of cyber weapons, with some nations such as the United States, China, Russia, and Israel possessing the most sophisticated cyber warheads.[28] Experience with norm development for emerging-technology weapons indicates that states with powerful cyber weapons are more likely to resist the emergence of any constraining norms. This is especially true with strong bureaucratic actors, such as the National Security Agency in the United States or the Federal Agency of Government Communications and Information in Russia, potentially advocating for permissive norms. While the Russians have been major advocates in the UN for a total prohibition on cyber weapons, their interest may be driven by a perception that the United States is the dominant cyber power or, perhaps more cynically, it could be akin to the Soviet Union's disingenuous early promotion of the constraining biological weapon and nuclear norms while simultaneously pursuing biological and nuclear weapons.

Regardless, the varied rates of adoption and development of cyber capabilities indicates that there will be divergent perspectives on constraining norms, making consensus difficult.

Conclusion

Cyber warfare is still in its relative infancy, and there are multiple possibilities for how this new mode of warfare will evolve over the coming decades. However, reasonable conclusions can be drawn regarding the prospects for the emergence of a constraining norm for cyber warfare based on norm evolution theory for emerging-technology weapons.[29] The theory indicates there are many hurdles facing development of constraining norms for cyber warfare and predicts that if current trends continue, constraining norms for cyber warfare will have trouble emerging and may not ever reach a norm cascade. This is principally because powerful state actors are unlikely to perceive a convergence between a robust constraining norm and their self-interest. While the norm evolution theory for emerging-technology weapons predicts grim prospects for the evolution of constraining cyber norms, unfortunately the threat of cyber warfare is not diminishing. Realizing that constraining norms are unlikely to develop into a regime that could successfully manage and contain the threat is helpful as it allows policymakers to instead focus on more fruitful strategies for addressing this growing threat.

Notes

1. James R. Clapper, "Statement for the Record: Worldwide Threat Assessment of the US Intelligence Community," March 12, 2013, https://www.dni.gov/files/documents/Intelligence%20Reports/2013%20ATA%20SFR%20for%20SSCI%2012%20Mar%202013.pdf.
2. James Forsyth and Billy Pope, "Structural Causes and Cyber Effects: Why International Order Is Inevitable in Cyberspace," *Strategic Studies Quarterly*, Winter 2014, 113–30.
3. John Norris, *Early Gunpowder Artillery: 1300–1600* (Wiltshire, UK: Crowood Press, 2003).
4. Martha Finnemore and Kathryn Sikkink, "International Norm Dynamics and Political Change," *International Organization* 52, no. 4 (1998): 887–917.
5. These include challenges of attribution following their use, attractiveness to weaker powers and non-state actors as asymmetric weapons, use as a force multiplier for conventional military operations, questionable deterrence value, target and weapon unpredictability, potential for major collateral damage or unintended consequences due to "borderless" domains, multiuse nature of the associated technologies, and the frequent use of covert programs to develop such weapons. Gregory Koblentz and Brian Mazanec, "Viral Warfare: The Security Implications of Cyber and Biological Weapons," *Comparative Strategy* 32, no. 5 (November 2013): 418–34.
6. Brian Mazanec, *The Evolution of Cyber War: International Norms for Emerging Technology Weapons* (Lincoln, NE: Potomac Books, 2015).
7. William Wan and Ellen Nakashima, "Report Ties Cyberattacks on U.S. Computers to Chinese Military," *Washington Post*, February 19, 2013, http://articles.washingtonpost.com/2013-02-19/world/37166888_1_chinese-cyber-attacks-extensive-cyber-espionage-chinese-military-unit; and U.S. Department of Justice Office of Public Affairs, "U.S. Charges Five Chinese Military Hackers for Cyber Espionage against U.S. Corporations and a Labor Organization for Commercial Advantage," May 19, 2014, https://www.justice.gov/opa/pr/us-charges-five-chinese-military-hackers-cyber-espionage-against-us-corporations-and-labor.
8. Anna Mulrine, "China Is a Lead Cyberattacker of U.S. Military Computers, Pentagon Reports," *Christian Science Monitor*, May 18, 2012, http://www.csmonitor.com/USA/Mil

itary/2012/0518/China-is-a-lead-cyberattacker-of-US-military-computers-Pentagon-reports.

9. Associated Press, "China Already Violating U.S. Cyberagreement, Group Says," October 19, 2015, http://www.cbsnews.com/news/crowdstrike-china-violating-cyberagreement-us-cyberespionage-intellectual-property/.
10. "Letter dated 12 September 2011 from the Permanent Representatives of China, the Russian Federation, Tajikistan, and Uzbekistan to the United Nations addressed to the Secretary-General," United Nations, A/66/359, September 14, 2011. https://ccdcoe.org/sites/default/files/documents/UN-110912-CodeOfConduct_0.pdf.
11. Roland Heickerö, "Emerging Cyber Threats and Russian Views on Information Warfare and Information Operationsm," *Swedish Defence Research Agency* (2010): 27.
12. Jason Healey, "How Emperor Alexander Militarized American Cyberspace," *Foreign Policy,* November 22, 2013. http://www.foreignpolicy.com/articles/2013/11/06/how_emperor_alexander_militarized_american_cyberspace?wp_login_redirect=0#sthash.63nueywc.dEQQ8Uxd.dpbs.
13. "International Strategy for Cyberspace: Prosperity, Security, and Openness in a Networked World," White House, May 2011, https://www.whitehouse.gov/sites/default/files/rss_viewer/international_strategy_for_cyberspace.pdf, 14; and Ellen Nakashima, "In Cyberwarfare, Rules of Engagement Still Hard to Define," *Washington Post,* March 10, 2013. http://www.washingtonpost.com/world/national-security/in-cyberwarfare-rules-of-engagement-still-hard-to-define/2013/03/10/0442507c-88da-11e2-9d71-f0feafdd1394_story.html.
14. William J. Lynn III, "The Pentagon's Cyberstrategy, One Year Later," *Foreign Affairs,* September 28, 2011.
15. Such as coherence and grafting with existing norms; permanently establishing a norm before the weapon exists or is fully capable or widespread; and threat inflation regarding the possible effects of the weapon, often by the private sector via industry and lobbying groups. In addition, the idea a weapon cannot be defended against will fuel interest in a norm; unitary dominance of a single actor with the particular weapon type gives that actor significant influence in norm emergence for that weapon type; and delays in proliferation (often due to technological barriers) can create added time for a constraining norm to emerge.
16. Martha Finnemore, "Cultivating International Cyber Norms," in *America's Cyber Future: Security and Prosperity in the Information Age,* ed. Kristin M. Lord and Travis Sharp (Center for a New American Security, June 2011), 99.
17. Michael M. Schmitt, ed. *Tallinn Manual on the International Law Applicable to Cyber Warfare* (Cambridge: Cambridge University Press, 2013).
18. Gary Brown and Keira Poellet, "The Customary International Law of Cyberspace," *Strategic Studies Quarterly* (Fall 2012): 141.
19. Based on author's analysis of James Lewis, "Significant Cyber Events since 2006," *Center for Strategic and International Studies,* July 11, 2013. https://csis-prod.s3.amazonaws.com/s3fs-public/160824_Significant_Cyber_Events_List.pdf.
20. Thomas Rid, *Cyber War Will Not Take Place* (Oxford: Hurst Publishers, Oxford University Press, April 2012).
21. Thomas Rid, "Cyberwar and Peace: Hacking Can Reduce Real-World Violence," *Foreign Affairs,* November–December 2013, http://www.foreignaffairs.com/articles/140160/thomas-rid/cyberwar-and-peace.
22. Erik Gartzke, "The Myth of Cyberwar: Bringing War in Cyberspace Back Down to Earth," *International Security* 38, no. 2 (Fall 2013): 42.
23. "Cyber Security Market Worth 202.36 Billion USD by 2021," *Markets and Markets,* http://www.marketsandmarkets.com/PressReleases/cyber-security.asp.
24. Bruce Schneier, "Threat of 'Cyberwar' Has Been Hugely Hyped," CNN, July 7, 2010. http://www.cnn.com/2010/OPINION/07/07/schneier.cyberwar.hyped/.
25. Jerry Brito and Tate Watkins, "Loving the Cy-

ber Bomb? The Dangers of Threat Inflation in Cybersecurity Policy," Mercatus Center, George Mason University, April 26, 2011, http://mercatus.org/publication/loving-cyber-bomb-dangers-threat-inflation-cybersecurity-policy; and "Is Cyberwar Hype Fuelling a Cybersecurity-Industrial Complex?," *Russia Today*, February 16, 2012, http://rt.com/usa/security-us-cyber-threat-529/.

26. Department of Defense, Defense Science Board Task Force Report, *Resilient Military Systems and the Advanced Cyber Threat*, January 2013, 1, http://www.acq.osd.mil/dsb/reports/ResilientMilitarySystems.CyberThreat.pdf.
27. Nicole Perlroth, "In Cyberattack on Saudi Firm, U.S. Sees Iran Firing Back," *New York Times*, October 23, 2012, http://www.nytimes.com/2012/10/24/business/global/cyberattack-on-saudi-oil-firm-disquiets-us.html.
28. As evidenced by the examination of customary state practice of cyber warfare reviewed earlier in this article.
29. Forsyth and Pope, "Structural Causes and Cyber Effects," 123.

GEORGETOWN

AVAILABLE NOW!

Spy Sites of Washington, DC
A Guide to the Capital Region's Secret History
Robert Wallace and H. Keith Melton
With Henry R. Schlesinger
978-1-62616-376-8, paperback, $24.95
978-1-62616-382-9, ebook, $24.95

Exporting Security
International Engagement, Security Cooperation, and the Changing Face of the US Military
Derek S. Reveron
978-1-62616-332-4, paperback, $32.95
978-1-62616-269-3, hardcover, $64.95
978-1-62616-333-1, ebook, $32.95

American Power and Liberal Order
A Conservative Internationalist Grand Strategy
Paul D. Miller
978-1-62616-342-3, hardcover, $32.95
978-1-62616-343-0, ebook, $32.95

Crude Strategy
Rethinking the US Military Commitment to Defend Persian Gulf Oil
Charles L. Glaser and Rosemary A. Kelanic, Editors
978-1-62616-335-5, paperback, $32.95
978-1-62616-334-8, hardcover, $64.95
978-1-62616-336-2, ebook, $32.95

Arab Fall
How the Muslim Brotherhood Won and Lost Egypt in 891 Days
Eric Trager
978-1-62616-362-1, hardcover, $32.95
978-1-62616-363-8, ebook, $32.95

Asia-Pacific Security
An Introduction
Joanne Wallis and Andrew Carr, Editors
978-1-62616-345-4, paperback, $34.95
978-1-62616-344-7, hardcover, $69.95
978-1-62616-346-1, ebook, $34.95

The Federal Management Playbook
Leading and Succeeding in the Public Sector
Ira Goldstein
Foreword by Tom Davis, former US Congressman
978-1-62616-372-0, paperback, $19.95
978-1-62616-381-2, ebook, $19.95
Public Management and Change series

AVAILABLE AS EBOOKS FROM SELECT EBOOK RETAILERS.

FOLLOW US @GUPRESS